BASEBALL'S
FORGOTTEN
BASICS

HOW TO ORDER THIS BOOK

BY PHONE: 866-401-4337 or 717-290-1660, 9AM–5PM Eastern Time

BY FAX: 717-509-6100

BY MAIL: Order Department

DEStech Publications, Inc.

1148 Elizabeth Avenue #2

Lancaster, PA 17601, U.S.A.

BY CREDIT CARD: American Express, VISA, MasterCard

BY WWW SITE: http://www.destechpub.com

BASEBALL'S
FORGOTTEN
BASICS

A Field Manual and Instructional DVD
For Coaches, Parents and Players

by Marc Shoenfelt

DES*tech* Publications, Inc.

Baseball's Forgotten Basics

DEStech Publications, Inc.
1148 Elizabeth Avenue #2
Lancaster, Pennsylvania 17601 U.S.A.

Printed in the United States of America
10   9   8   7   6   5   4   3

Main entry under title:
    Baseball's Forgotten Basics: A Field Manual and Instructional DVD

A DEStech Publications book
Bibliography: p.
Includes index p. 167

Library of Congress Catalog Card No. 2005936225
ISBN No. 978-1-932078-53-4

Preface   *ix*

Chapter 1—**Coaching Tips: Remembering Who You Are** . . 1
You Are a Role Model   1
You Are a Teacher   4
You Are a Parent   6
You Are an Inspiration   7
You Are a Coach   9
Al Jordan   12

Chapter 2—**Stretching and Strengthening the Arm** 13
Hiding the Baseballs   13
The Rotator Cuff   14
Glove Stretches   14
Elbow Stretches   17
Surgical Tubing   18
Buddy Stretch   20
Summary   21

Chapter 3—**Throwing a Baseball** 23
Catch Not Fetch   23
Grip   24
Playing Catch   27
Fixing Throwing Mechanics   32
Summary   37

Chapter 4—**Hitting** 39
On-deck/Mental Approach   40
Phase I: Stance/Pre-flight Check   41
Phase II: The Launch Position (loading up)   48

Contents

Phase III: The Swing   51
Phase IV: The Follow-through   55
Bunting   57
Grip It and Rip It   60
Practice, Practice, Practice   60
Situational Hitting   60
The Winning Edge   61

Chapter 5—20 Hitting Flaws and How To Fix Them **63**
Phase I: The Stance   63
Phase II: Launch Position   67
Phase III: The Swing   71
Phase IV: The Follow-through   77
Fixing Hitting Problems: An Overview   80

Chapter 6—Infielding **81**
Mental Approach   81
Approach (Before the Ball is Fielded)   82
Fielding the Ball   84
Throwing the Ball   86
Backhands and Forehands   88
Relays from the Outfield   91
Summary   93

Chapter 7—Turning the Double Play **95**
Shortstop   95
Second Baseman   98
First and Third Base   100
Taking the Feed at Second Base   101
Tips and Drills for Turning the Double Play   102
Summary   105

Chapter 8—Outfield Play **107**
Catching a Fly Ball   107
Fly Ball Communication   109
Ground Balls to the Outfield   111
Throwing from the Outfield   112
Balls at the Fence   112
Summary   113

Chapter 9—12 Defensive Drills and Games for
Infielders and Outfielders **115**
Infield Drills   115
Outfield Drills   118
Summary   120

Contents

Chapter 10—**Pitching**. **121**
    Safety/Pitch Count   121
    Mechanics   123
    Off-speed Pitches   128
    Drills   130
    Summary   132

Chapter 11—**Nine Pitching Flaws and How
           to Fix Them** **135**
    Pitching Flaws   135
    Summary   141

Chapter 12—**Base Running**. **143**
    On-Deck   143
    Home to First   144
    Stealing   147
    Sliding   150
    First to Third Base Running   152
    Rounding Third   152
    Games and Drills   153
    Summary   154

Chapter 13—**Practice Management** **155**
    Before the First Practice   155
    First Practice   156
    First 25 Minutes of Practice   157
    Batting Practice   158
    Defense Management   161
    Pitching   162
    Practice Time   163
    Conditioning vs. Base Running   163
    Practice Schedule Model   163
    Summary   165
    Practice Checklist   165

Index   *167*

About the Author   *171*

I love baseball. My dream growing up was like many kids' . . . I wanted to play major league baseball. I used to eat baseballs with my cereal in the morning and go to sleep at night with my glove. To become a major leaguer, you need to possess incredible athletic ability and keen eye-hand coordination, not to mention the basic fundamentals of the game. There are crucial intangibles that help even things out if you are lacking any of those qualities. They are work habits, fortitude, hustle, and instincts, to name a few. These qualities helped me have a successful collegiate career. After my last game at the college world series, life had other plans. I became an elementary school teacher, and just as important eight years later, a teacher of the game I love.

What qualities make an effective baseball teacher? Does a major leaguer really know how he hits that ball 500 feet, or is he just blessed with the physical talent? Have you ever read a book from your favorite baseball player and wanted more applicable drills or information?

Teaching young kids is a difficult task and requires huge doses of patience and skill. When I decided to start my baseball business, B2B Baseball, I set out to teach the fundamentals in a way that all coaches, parents, and kids could understand. I knew two things. For the past nine years, I taught children with many different ways of learning and did so effectively. Second, I knew the fundamentals of baseball and taught them with positive results. I started a youth baseball training program to focus on equipping coaches with the know-how to teach kids baseball. I set out on a mission to reach as many coaches, kids, and even parents, as possible. This book and DVD are part of that mission.

Baseball is a simple game, loved and cherished by millions. At some point since the sport's conception, the baseball world has gotten caught up in so much theory that we forgot the game is played based on simple fundamentals. This book sets out to accomplish two things: to pepper you with the basic fundamentals and ways to teach them, and to bring what's described in the book to life through a DVD companion. For learners of baseball, this is a powerful combination. The book explains in words each and every concept, and the DVD shows coaches and players the skills in motion. Whether you are a seasoned veteran, or a new coach trying to learn the latest drills, this book will be an eye-opener for the ways you approach your next practice or game.

May you eat baseballs with your cereal and go to sleep with your glove!

CHAPTER 1

Coaching Tips:
Remembering Who You Are

WHEN I set out to write a field manual, I knew I needed to devote a chapter to more than just the fundamentals of the game. Baseball, like all sports, is a microcosm of life. We are shaped and molded by the decisions we make on and off the field. As a coach or an instructor, you will be remembered by your players as a role model, teacher, parent figure, and mentor for the rest of their lives.

When I was growing up, one of my idols was my youth baseball coach, Al Jordan. I hung on every word he said on the field and worshiped the ground he walked on. At the time, he was the greatest baseball mind I had ever known. In reality, he probably didn't know baseball any more than each and every parent in the stands. He was a blue-collar guy who volunteered his time to coach little league baseball for a season. Yes, Al was an ordinary man, but he was blessed with an extraordinary gift. His gift was that he inspired me to feel like I had a chance to be a major leaguer. Along the way, he made a positive, immeasurable impact on me, as well as on the other players on the team. What made Al such a great little league coach? The rest of this chapter will show you just why he and others like him have been successful and influential.

You Are a Role Model

Have you ever run into one of your players off the baseball field, at church, or in a supermarket? If you have, you probably got the look of "What are you doing here . . . aren't you supposed to be at the field?" Your players look up to you and perceive you as

1

superhuman. They think you sleep in the dugout and eat dinner at the concession stand. With this in mind, there are certain characteristics you should display both on and off the field.

Watch Your Language

Good words point to good character, and vice-verse. I am not talking about profanity. Your words and the way you address certain situations are paramount. The last thing a kid wants to hear from you is that he made a mistake and is wrong. *In all situations,* your tone should be positive. Mistakes kids make should turn into a learning experience, not a traumatic one.

Watch Your Body Language

We don't give young people enough credit when it comes to being perceptive and understanding situations. Let me paint a picture for you. A ground ball is hit to your shortstop, and he commits an error. You, as the coach, yell, "It's okay, nice try. You'll get it next time," while clapping your hands in encouragement. By all accounts you did a good job of encouraging the player—verbally. When a kid boots the ball, what's the first thing he does after committing the error? He looks at you the coach, or his parents. The first few seconds of this look are important, not just for how you as the coach are speaking, but also for what your body is saying. Did you as the coach look down at the ground? Shake your head in disapproval? Kick the dirt? Sometimes it is not what we say that makes the first and lasting impression. All of these actions affirm that the kid messed up, he is bad, and you as the coach are not pleased with him. It is tough to control, but keeping your body language positive is imperative in situations like this.

Some positive expressions are: to nod your head to affirm you understand and can relate, or clap your hands and explain what to do with the ball if it's hit to the player again. Always redirecting actions in a positive way and reacting positively will boost the morale of your players after an unintentional mistake.

Don't Argue with the Umpire

One of the biggest blunders by youth coaches today is arguing with the umpire. Maybe those doing the jawing grew up watching

Earl Weaver, Billy Martin, or other professionals throwing bats or getting in the face of the men in blue. THIS IS YOUTH BASEBALL! Set an example by supporting the umpires. They are volunteering their time and are trying to get the call right. Do they make mistakes? Never! (Just kidding.) If you feel you must discuss a call with an umpire, refrain from raising your voice or making a scene. It is embarrassing for you, the umpire, the kids, and the parents in the stands. Take time between innings or after the game to discuss a problem you may have. At these times, the tone of the conversation can be slower, and the dialogue civil.

Smile

Looking at some coaches may lead you to believe that scowling and being grumpy are prerequisites for being a youth baseball coach. This is baseball . . . America's pastime. The game is supposed to be fun, so model the fun and enjoy it yourself. Let's not lose kids to other sports because adult instructors forgot that baseball is fun to play. I love going to a baseball game and watching the coach smile and laugh with the kids. Laughter truly is contagious. So, show those pearly whites and let your kids know that you are having a good time too.

Raise Expectations for Parents Too

The vulgar and inconsiderate fan can poison the atmosphere of any event, especially games played by children. You, as a coach, can have an effect on your parents at games. Here is what you should do. Before the first practice, a meeting should be held or a letter sent home outlining the guidelines for the upcoming season. In those guidelines or meeting, stress to your parents the importance of being supportive and not disruptive at games. Explain that you are not going to yell or argue calls, and you expect the same in return from the parents. If they do have a concern, ask them to speak with you after the game or practice. What if the parent still decides to heckle the opponent or scream at his kid? I would tell the parents before the first practice that you, as the coach, are going to leave the dugout and ask the parent to leave the premises. Stress how this would be an embarrassment you don't want, and obviously they don't want. You will gain support and respect from your parents, if you actually enforce such an important rule. Its purpose is to ensure that all can enjoy the game.

You Are a Teacher As much as you are there to shape and mold the kids into outstanding baseball players, you are also there to teach them more important lessons about life and character. I would rather have my own child on a team guided by a person of character and discipline than on a team led by a former player possessing intimate knowledge of the game but few clear ideals. Teaching the skills is important, as you will soon see. However, the lessons learned playing youth sports reach far beyond the baseball diamond.

Winning is Not the Only Thing

Winning is important. Anyone who tells you otherwise is either kidding themselves or should not be in a sport that keeps score. It is, however, not the only thing (contrary to the quote from the late Vince Lombardi). Important lessons for life are learned from losing. In the age we live in, judging a coach by the number of wins and losses becomes the deciding factor in whom we want our children to play for. I argue that winning and losing at a young age does not equate to winning and losing at older ages. For those who played youth baseball, think about when you were younger. How many of the best baseball players in your youth league went on to play at a higher level in baseball, let alone make the high school team? Teaching the skills and drills and instilling a love and passion for the game are still at the top of my list of priorities when it comes to a youth coach. Teaching your kids to win is important. But an even more important lesson is to teach them to lose with class, dignity, and sportsmanship. Learning from your mistakes and "getting them next time" are as important to a healthy mindset as wanting to win.

Fundamentals, Fundamentals, Fundamentals

Teaching the fundamentals should be at the core of every coach's repertoire. Baseball has thrived on its simplicity and unchanged fundamentals. When I do a seminar, most people expect me to pull out a magic wand and demonstrate advanced drills and techniques that will make their kid into a miniature Alex Rodriguez. They inevitably discover there are many things to learn—counting only the fundamentals. Advanced information can often not be taught and comprehended until a child is older.

Every coach, no matter what his or her level, should be equipped with the knowledge of the fundamentals. With the help of what I demonstrate here and on the DVD, you will learn the drills that imprint the fundamentals. It takes doing an action one thousand times perfectly for it to settle into muscle-motor memory. One thousand times! In the fast-food era we live in, how many kids and coaches do you know who can withstand that type of monotony and persistence? Once a player is fundamentally sound, she can work on the physical training necessary to become a superior athlete. Watch the Little League World Series. How many times do the participants make an error? They hit pitches coming in at speeds equivalent to major league fastballs! With sound fundamentals and mechanics being established among your coaches and players, you will see your program begin to produce solid baseball players, from top to bottom.

Sportsmanship

Being a good sport is paramount. It is one of the best concepts you can teach players. Here are a few (of many) examples.

First, don't heckle your opponents. The old chant "We want a pitcher not a belly itcher" should be thrown into the archives with the rest of those types of comments. Reinforce to your players that you should only be positive and encourage others to do their best. Often a coach gets all wrapped up in his own agenda and forgets that the other team is full of kids too. How many times do you help a kid on the other team if he is doing something wrong? Wishing that the opposing pitcher will keep walking your kids falls into the category of bad sportsmanship. If a kid on the opposing team is doing something mechanically wrong, help him. Maybe you see something the opposing coach does not see. There isn't a better way to model sportsmanship, in my mind. That same child may be playing alongside one of your kids when he gets older, or better yet, may be on one of your future teams.

Speak at Their Level

Too often we want to impress people with how much we know

instead of teaching them what they need to know. Remember to speak to kids at their level. Throwing out big words and baseball jargon is meaningless. As you will see throughout this book, coming up with simple words to explain complicated processes is key in relaying your knowledge to your ballplayers.

Being six feet, two inches tall, I imagine I am a giant in the eyes of most youth baseball players. Actually, the height of an adult can be intimidating and gives the illusion of speaking down from on high. You are much more effective if you lower your eye level to the players. Kneeling or bending over while talking to your players helps put you and your message on the same level as your listeners.

Lastly, lecturing or giving a mini-clinic to explain skills is boring and ineffective. A good teacher will incorporate games and activities that not only explain, but engage each and every kid in fun activities. There is nothing more tedious to a young kid than sitting and listening to an adult talk about the finer points of pitching mechanics. Use games and drills to teach concepts, and baseball practice will be better and more enjoyable.

You Are a Parent   Unless you are a die-hard fan living out a dream to coach, chances are you are a parent with a son or daughter on the team. This can be a sensitive issue when certain predicaments arise. Even if you are not a parent, each and every kid on the team looks up to you. It is important to treat every child as though he or she is your own.

Equal Playing Time

If you are playing youth baseball, there is nothing more boring than sitting on the bench. Each and every kid should get playing time in a game no matter what the situation may be. In saying that, you may also have a child on the team. Do me a favor. For the first game of the year, sit your son or daughter on the bench for the first two or three innings. Why? It will send a message that everyone is going to get equal playing time, and you will not show favoritism. If you don't have a child on the team, consider sitting the best player. Think about it. When would you rather have your good players in anyway . . . at the beginning of the game, or the end?

Post-Game Breakdown

After the game is over, like most adults, you want to replay the game in your mind and analyze each and every situation. Kids want to go home and ride their bike or play with their video games. No sooner is the game over, and kids are running around with the players from the other team and doing something else. Most kids do not want to relive the game. On the ride home, don't bring up the events of the game. If your son or daughter initiates the conversation, then you are more than welcome to review the game's events. In more cases than not, the boy or girl will want to talk about something else, and you should, too.

Listen to Your Spouse

I am saying this as a married man. When your spouse tells you something or gives you advice, listen. Remember, he or she is also a parent on your team and sees your actions from the stands. Your better half is sitting among other parents and watching every move and action you make. Your better half can be a good resource for critiquing your coaching technique. Mom or Dad, even a grandparent, may just turn out to be your best assistant coach.

Encourage when You are Losing

It is easy to encourage kids and be positive when you are winning. How about losing? Putting your head down and crossing your arms are not options when the chips are stacked against you. This is when you earn your coaching stripes. Keeping the morale up in the dugout and getting the kids not to quit are two characteristics you can help foster when the going gets tough and the team is losing. Too many times coaches concede defeat and separate themselves from the team emotionally.

It is Not Your Childhood; It is Theirs

If you are a coach who didn't make his high school team or have unfinished business from your playing days, this is not the time for you to redeem your lost glory. It is about the kids. When I come to a game, I want to see the kids play baseball. More times than I can count, I see the coach or hear the coach's voice from the

You Are an Inspiration

7

dugout. Games should be kid directed, practices coach directed. I am not saying that there shouldn't be teachable moments or encouraging remarks during games. However, you, the coach, ranting, raving or becoming a spectacle is not what people came to observe. It is a time for you to inspire kids to be the best that they can, and your job is to make that happen.

How do you inspire kids? Each and every player on the team wants to be told they are doing well and have the ability to be great one day. There are those who may not possess the physical ability to become major leaguers, but in their eyes they don't know that, and your job is not to reveal it to them. Making them believe they have the ability, and encouraging them to be the best they can be is a good start in what is a quest for every young kid who plays youth baseball. Remember, there was a youth basketball coach long ago who thought Michael Jordan didn't have the ability to make the team, and another who thought Scottie Pippen should be an equipment manager.

Each Kid is Special and is Important

Whether the best player on the team, or the worst, each and every child must feel he is an important part of the team. Frequently we focus on what children are doing wrong and do not compliment or remark about the things they are doing right. You will get much more satisfaction when you take the worst player on the team and point out something she did right and make an example of it. It not only boosts self-confidence, but it also goes a long way with peers. Now the player is accepted and is the one who coach pointed out is doing something right.

Don't Yell or Raise Your Voice when Teaching or Correcting

Screaming and yelling does not inspire students. Instead, this behavior makes them want to rebel and not want to deal with you again. Nobody wants a yeller or a screamer as a coach. There are more effective ways to let your players know something was unacceptable or done incorrectly. Most of the time coaches may not even know that their voices are raised. Adrenaline, nerves, or competitiveness may creep in and take over. An example in its worst form is when you single out a specific player and proceed to give him a tongue-lashing. A better way to handle it would be to pull him away from his peers and calmly discuss the problem. I have encountered other coaches and parents who think yelling has merit. The more you yell, the higher you climb in the coaching ranks among certain kids and parents. To them, it means you care and are better. To me, screaming makes you unworthy to coach and someone who should not be in front of young kids or instructing them.

Play Kids at All Positions

When I do clinics, inevitably I will have a young man who comes up and tells me that he only plays third base or pitches. He is shocked when I tell him that today he is going to learn to hit the cutoff man when throwing from the outfield.

Let's say you are in a youth league with approximately 200 youth players between the ages of 9 to12 playing baseball (this may be more than one league in some areas but they all go to the same school district). Only nine of them will be starting for your high school team in a couple of years and five or six more might be on the bench. Chances are if you are playing shortstop for your youth team, you will be not be at that position in high school (unless you are the best player in your district). Play kids at as many positions as possible when they are young. The more positions a kid can play in high school, the better chance that kid has to make the team.

Communicate, Communicate, Communicate

Nobody likes to be kept in the dark about anything. Life would be much easier if everyone learned to communicate openly and honestly and ideas were explained in detail. You can take this and apply it directly to the way you run your team. Before the season, send each and every player on your team a letter explaining in detail your expectations, the schedule, practice times, etc. Kids love to get mail!

Next, telephone the parents of your players as a follow-up. Share the same points from the letter and your philosophy on coaching, along with any other "adult" issues. When the season starts and the first practice comes, it is time to play baseball. The practice can start more smoothly because expectations and guidelines are already established.

In school, the instructor always gives the kids an objective for each lesson. You too should explain your objective for each practice. Start each practice with a quick overview of what the players are going to learn. It will save a lot of questions throughout the practice ("Coach, what are we doing next?") and gives you a "lesson plan." When the practice is over, revisit what you wanted the kids to learn and check for understanding. In the teaching profession, we call this "KWL":

What do you **K**now?
What we **W**ant you to learn?
What did you **L**earn?

The bottom line is, the more you communicate in all facets with your players and parents, the smoother and more enjoyable a season you will have. Don't ever assume your players know what you mean, and emphasize the only dumb question is the one that is not asked.

Dealing with Parents

Sometimes dealing with parents is more difficult than dealing with kids. Although a separate book needs to be written on this topic, here are a few suggestions on specific problems.

We've already stressed communicating. For example, calling parents before the season and explaining your expectations and your philosophy for coaching. This cannot be emphasized enough.

I commonly get the question, "What do you do with a parent who chronically drops off their kid ten minutes late for no apparent reason?" That's easy. If you say practice starts at 6 P.M., then start it at that time. Not one minute later. When the parent shows up to drop off their kid next time, they will see that practice has already started and will hopefully show up a little before 6 P.M.

Next suggestion, give upset parents a chance to speak. Shouting solves nothing and not letting them speak creates problems. We all like to blow off a little steam . . . let them express their concerns and listen. Somebody smart once said, "You can attract more flies with honey than vinegar".

Know Your Kids

When you read this heading you probably thought to yourself, "Who does this guy think he is? Of course I know who my kids are." Knowing the children means having an idea of each one's health needs and each boy and girl's way of learning. You should have an emergency phone list in case a kid on your team gets hurt. How about allergies? It is very important before the season starts that you create a reference in case of medical issues. An injury (or two) is bound to happen at some point during the season. Instead of panicking and waiting for that situation to arise, do yourself a favor and create a phone list with notes.

Another way you should get to know your players is by understanding their learning styles. Some kids learn fast, others take more time. Some respond better to constructive criticism, others need more praise. Instead of adopting a hard-nose, no-nonsense approach for everyone (or the opposite), get to know the learning style for each and every player. It will make you a much more effective coach and teacher of the game.

Do You Know What You Signed Up For?

A typical youth league season encompasses approximately 15 weeks of your year. Break that down into practices and games, plus meetings, evaluations, travel time, team functions, work detail on the fields, etc. You will be spending numerous hours— and perhaps a few dollars—on a position for which you volunteered. Make sure you understand what coaching involves before you volunteer. People coach for many reasons. Your motive should be to make a difference in a kid's life or something very similar . . . period.

Organize Your Practices

Showing up to practice with a game plan is essential. Disorganized practices begin with something like this: "Coach, what are we doing tonight?" The coach responds, "I don't know . . . maybe we'll hit a little and then take some infield and outfield". Sound familiar? Practice should be a structured event with all kids engaged actively the entire practice. Attend a practice at any level from little league to high school and you will rarely see every kid engaged. Chapter 13 will show you how to manage a practice from beginning to end.

Get Educated

You are doing your players and yourself a disservice if you choose not to educate yourself about baseball. I am not talking about baseball trivia either. Learning the latest skills and drills from watching the Wednesday night game of the week on TV is not too beneficial either. Attend a clinic, rent a video, or read a good book on the topic. This should be something everyone wants to do. I am finding out, however, that most coaches choose not to do any of these. Life is a learning process, and so is coaching baseball. Become like a sponge and soak in as many drills or games to make you a more effective coach.

Al Jordan Following all of the recommendations above will help guide you in becoming "Al Jordan" to your players. Al didn't implement all of the ideas above, but his intentions and coaching skills made a lasting impression on the players he coached. After applying these concepts to your coaching repertoire, my hope is that your players will think of you as highly as I think of Al Jordan. My love for baseball was enhanced by the love and compassion he had for this beautiful game, and the way he treated his parents and players.

CHAPTER 2

Stretching and Strengthening
the Arm

THE number one injury in sports today is to the throwing shoulder. With that fact in mind, you must use specific exercises to help your players stretch and strengthen their arms to reduce the risk of injury.

There is no better time to learn and apply these exercises than in youth baseball. Taking care of the arm at an early age, when a player's arm is the most susceptible to injury, will build strength and prolong the ability to play the game. The throwing motion is one of the fastest movements the human body can perform. The speed and exertion the throwing arm goes through puts unbelievable stress on the shoulder. To handle the stress, a player needs to build the muscles and get the shoulder warm to prevent injury.

Hiding the Baseballs

Here's an experiment. Before players arrive at the field, hide the baseballs. The players will run around in a frenzy looking for something to throw. Last year I held a clinic for a youth league, which was preceded by a coaching clinic. At the coaching clinic, I told the coaches I was going to hide the baseballs before the players arrived. I promised them that somehow, some way, the players would find an object to throw before the clinic started. After arriving, the players went on a frantic hunt for a baseball. When no ball was found, they stood a few feet from one another and threw their gloves back and forth!

Throwing a ball as the first activity of a practice is a habit that should be changed. A sprinter doesn't show up at the track, get on his mark, and run hard. The sprinter stretches the legs and trots

This symbol indicates reference to Companion DVD for video instruction

13

slowly to loosen them before running hard. A weightlifter doesn't put 350 lbs. on the bar and begin doing presses. He stretches the upper body and begins with a light load on the bar, gradually working his way up to a heavier weight. So why does a baseball player show up at the field and perform one of the fastest movements possible by the human body before stretching?

The Rotator Cuff Damage occurs because players do not warm up the arm and stretch it before throwing. The traditional movements of taking the arm across the front of the body or over the head do not do an adequate job. Not only does the arm need to be loosened, but also the shoulder, which contains four tiny muscles that in turn form the rotator cuff. Exercises described in this chapter stretch and strengthen the rotator cuff.*

There are a number of ways to stretch the arm. While any one is beneficial, a combination of several will help a player build strength in the arm. Strengthening the arm is important, and proper mechanics need to be learned in conjunction with the exercises to reduce the risk of injury.

Glove Stretches Glove stretches are easy to do, require no fancy gadgets, and the players can perform them on their own. As the name implies, players hold a glove in their throwing arm and move it as a weight. This loosens the arm and builds strength in the rotator cuff. Glove stretches should be done for a total of five minutes.

When doing the exercises, make sure to isolate the throwing shoulder. The rest of the body should remain still as the throwing shoulder moves during the drills. Here are ways to help young players reduce body motion. Encourage the players to stand tall and keep their feet together. The non-throwing arm should drape across the chest, similar to the arm's location when saluting the flag. In this stance, the trunk cannot easily move, and the non-throwing shoulder remains still. Moving the torso or the non-throwing shoulder diminishes the effect of the drills on the throwing arm.

---

*If you want a more advanced explanation of the medical and biomechanical nuances of the arm, read the excellent book *Saving the Pitcher* by Will Carroll. He breaks down the reasons for arm injuries and provides detailed reasons for proper mechanics and conditioning.

Stretches

The following stretches can be done in any order. Do each exercise for eight to ten repetitions while holding a glove in the throwing hand. When the exercises are complete, the arm will be a little tired and really loose to begin throwing. The stretches were inspired by the Jobe exercises, named for Dr. Frank Jobe, the orthopedic surgeon who pioneered Tommy John surgery. The original movements were first intended to rehabilitate arms after surgery, but are now a part of daily routines used by major league pitchers.

Glove stretches should be done slowly and in a controlled manner. All except one of the stretches are done with the arm fully extended.

Stretch #1—Windmills Forward

See Section 2.1

With the throwing arm outstretched to the side, large circles are made in a forward direction.

Stretch #2—Windmills Backward

See Section 2.2

With the throwing arm outstretched to the side, large circles are made in a backward direction.

Stretch #3—Swing Over Head

See Section 2.3

For a right-hander, the glove should start around the left thigh. The arm will swing laterally toward the throwing arm side, extend up into the air, and end up behind the head. After finishing behind the head, the same path is taken back down to the thigh. On the last repetition, the elbow should be held behind the head with the non-throwing hand. The player should hold it there for about five seconds.

Stretch #4—Swing Across Chest

See Section 2.4

The throwing arm should be extended away from the body on the throwing side. The arm will come forward and end up on the left side of the body (for a right-hander). The arm is lying across the chest, with the glove touching the left shoulder. When the swing is complete, the arm should follow the same path until it reaches the starting point. On the last repetition, the arm can be held against the chest with the non-throwing hand for approximately five seconds.

See Section 2.5

Stretch #5—Circles in Front

For circles in front, the throwing arm should be extended straight out in front of the body, giving the appearance of pointing at something with the glove. The player makes small circles with her hand, clockwise or counterclockwise. After the maximum repetitions in one direction, the player switches to the other.

See Section 2.6

Stretch #6—Circles to the Side

The throwing arm should be extended from the body on the throwing side, as though you were pointing to the left or right. Small circles should be made in either direction, clockwise or counterclockwise. When the maximum repetitions have been met in one direction, the player reverses the direction for the same number of times.

See Section 2.7

Stretch #7—Circles Over the Head

With the arm extended over the head (like raising the hand to ask a question), the player makes small circles in either a clockwise or counterclockwise direction. When the maximum repetitions have been done, reverse the direction for the same number of reps.

See Section 2.8

Stretch #8—Arm Behind the Back

This is the only exercise that requires the player to bend the arm at the elbow (the arm will not be straight). The throwing arm needs to be placed behind the back. The non-throwing hand should clasp the wrist of the throwing arm and pull up. It is important the upper torso stays tall and doesn't bend at the waist. This position should just be held steady. No movement needs to be made. Hold the wrist and pull it up gently. The drill should be stopped immediately if pain or discomfort is felt.

Elbow Stretches

Stretch #9—Bent-over Circles

 *See Section 2.9*

For bent-over circles, the player needs to bend at the waist, and place the non-throwing elbow on the left knee (for a right-hander). The throwing arm should remain palm down, and the glove should almost touch the ground. The player then makes a large circle with the arm in either the clockwise or counter clockwise direction, as though stirring a pot. Once the maximum number of repetitions is met, the player should reverse the direction.

Stretch #10—Bent-over Throw-backs

See Section 2.10

The player bends at the waist, and places the non-throwing elbow on the left knee (for a right-hander). The throwing arm should be placed palm down, and the glove should almost touch the ground. The player then swings the glove in the air toward the throwing side of the body. The glove should end up behind the body and over the head. The same path is followed back down to the ground.

Stretch #11—Free Swinging

See Section 2.11

The player bends at the waist with both arms extended to the ground. The arms should swing from side to side, staying the same distance from one another throughout the swinging motion. Each time the arms swing, one arm should extend over the body and behind the back. This stretches out the arms, and also loosens the torso.

The elbow is the second most frequently injured body part, and should be stretched to prevent injury. The glove is not needed for the elbow stretches.

Elbow Stretches

Stretch #1—Palm Down, Pull Back Fingers

 *See Section 2.12*

Straighten the throwing arm out in front of the body palm down. With the non-throwing hand, bend the fingers back to stretch the ligaments in the forearm, which are those that extend into the elbow. Done properly, this stretch should be felt in the elbow region.

See Section 2.13

Stretch #2—Palm Up, Pull Down Fingers

With the throwing arm pointed in front of the body palm up, pull the fingers down. Make sure to keep the arm straight. This will stretch the ligaments that run into the biceps.

See Section 2.14

Stretch #3—Twist the Wrist

With the arm extended, palm up or palm down, twist the wrist with the non-throwing hand. It doesn't matter in which direction the hand is twisted, as long as the twist is done both to the left and to the right.

Surgical Tubing
There is no better way to stretch and strengthen the arm than by using surgical tubing, which is slowly pulled from a stationary object. While properly lifting weights has merit, pulling surgical tubing provides the best functional training to develop the throwing arm. The resistance from the surgical tube strengthens the shoulder safely without damaging the muscles. Surgical tubing is the first rehabilitative step for people who've had arm surgery, and orthopedic surgeons also prescribe tubing for patients with shoulder problems. Young players can benefit from keeping tubing with them at all times, and using the tool in the off-season to develop strength. The tubing can be tied to a chain link fence, railings, or a pole. Regularly using the tubing at the field will stretch the arm before throwing. There is special tubing on the market that has a baseball already tied at one end, but any tubing will work. Eight to ten repetitions are recommended when performing the following exercises. As with the glove exercises, the shoulder should be isolated and the torso held still. The movements should be slow and controlled. Usually the arm is kept straight. Here, the exercises are described for a right-hander.

See Section 2.15

Exercise #1—Front Raises

With the tube tied to a fixed object, the player faces the anchored tube. Next, grasp the tube with the throwing hand, and pull the tube straight up in the air and over the head. The hand will finish above the head, and return on the same path to the waist area.

Exercise #2—Pull-backs

See Section 2.16

The player faces the tube's anchored position for this exercise. The hand should start around the waist, with the arm straight and a little in front of the body. The tube needs to be pulled straight back behind the player, never going higher than the waist. Pull the tube as far back as possible, and return on the same path to complete one repetition.

Exercise #3—Lateral Pull-backs

See Section 2.17

Instead of facing the tube's anchoring point, the player turns ninety degrees to the right. The left shoulder is facing the anchored tube in this position. Starting with the right arm across the chest and hand around the left shoulder, the player pulls the tube across the body with the arm straight and finishes with the arm out to the right side of the body. The same path should be followed in reverse until the hand returns to the left shoulder.

Exercise #4—"L" Pushes

See Section 2.18

The player starts with his or her back toward the tube. Grabbing the tube, the player then places the arm in the "L" position. The arm should not be straight, but positioned so it forms an "L," as in the pitching motion (refer to Chapter 10 on pitching for the "L" position). The arm extends forward, with the hand finishing in front of the body. The path is then retraced until the arm is back in the "L" position.

Exercise #5—Reverse Raises

See Section 2.19

With the back toward the tube, the player grabs the tube with the arm extended toward the ground. The hand should be near the waist or right thigh. The tube is then pulled straight ahead and raised until the hand is at shoulder level. The same path should be followed until the arm is pointed straight down toward the ground.

Exercise #6—Lateral Front Pulls

See Section 2.20

While facing the tube, the player turns ninety degrees to the left, with the right shoulder facing the tube. The player should then grab the tube with the right hand. At this point the right arm is extended to the right at shoulder level. The left arm remains at the player's side. Starting straight, the right arm pulls the tube across the chest, and ends up on the left side of the body. The same path should be followed back to the original position on the right side of the body.

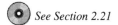 *See Section 2.21*

Exercise #7—Diagonal Raises

For the diagonal raise the tube is placed under the left foot. The throwing hand then grabs the other end of the tube and pulls up diagonally to the right. The arm should be straight, and the hand should end up over the head and out to the right. The same path is followed back down to the left thigh to complete the repetition.

Buddy Stretch The glove and surgical tubing stretches are great for players to do on their own. Buddy stretches should be done with an adult. If buddy stretches are done improperly, there is a risk of injury. For that reason, an adult needs to supervise and conduct the stretches. Buddy stretches improve a player's range of motion, while strengthening the rotator cuff. An improved range of motion reduces the risk of injury when a player throws the ball. Parental permission should be granted before a coach assists a player with the following stretches.

See Section 2.22

Stretch #1—"L" Position Stretch

With the player's throwing arm in the "L" position, the coach places his right hand on the player's elbow, while his left hand clasps the player's throwing hand. The coach places the right hand on the elbow to support the arm and keep it motionless. In a slow motion, the coach bends the throwing arm backward. The elbow should not move, and the player's body needs to stay erect and motionless. The coach gently takes the arm back until the player reaches his or her full range of motion. This exercise should never cause pain. When the full range of motion is reached, the coach holds the position for a ten count. Very slowly, the coach then returns the arm to the "L" position. The coach next takes the hand and pulls it forward, so the hand is facing the ground. The left hand now supports the elbow, and the right hand clasps the hand. The player's hand should be pulled backward until it reaches full range of motion. Once full range is reached, the coach should hold the position for a ten count. Very slowly, the coach then takes the arm back into the "L" position. The same sequence should be performed again, with the arm going back, and then the arm pointing down and the hand facing down and back. It is very important to do these exercises slowly. The second time the exercises are done, a significant increase in the range of motion will be evident. When players have done these exercises a number of times, the player can give resistance after the ten count to improve strength.

Stretch #2—Arm Behind Head

 *See Section 2.23*

The player's throwing arm should be pinned behind the head. The arm should be bent, with the elbow pointing straight up, and the hand facing the ground. Both elbow and hand will be behind the head, with the hand resting near the middle of the back. The coach gently pulls the elbow with her left hand, while her right hand grasps the player's wrist. The coach then pulls the elbow until the player has reached a full range of motion. Again, no pain should be felt. The purpose is to stretch the area below the shoulder into the back. The arm should be held for a ten count and released slowly. The exercise should be repeated and held for another ten count.

Stretch #3—Arm Behind Back

See Section 2.24

The throwing arm of the player is placed behind the back, with the forearm lying across the belt area. The coach places his or her left hand on the wrist of the player, and his or her right hand on the player's elbow. With the player standing erect, the coach pulls the wrist and elbow in the air slowly. Again, the player should not be in any discomfort. When the full range of motion is reached, the coach holds the position for a ten count. The coach then releases and slowly lowers the arm. The same exercise should be repeated and held for a ten count.

Summary

The stretches prescribed in this chapter will not only stretch the arm, but will build needed strength to throw a ball harder. Combined with error-free mechanics, the stretches will enable a player to throw harder for a longer period of time. Safety is the main concern. Routinely performing the stretches in this chapter will put a player on the path to a healthy future and greater throwing velocity.

CHAPTER 3

Throwing a Baseball

THROWING a baseball accurately is arguably the most important action in our sport. More games are lost in youth baseball due to either walks (pitcher can't throw strikes) or throwing errors (fielders' throws miss targets). You can win or develop a competitive youth baseball team if you teach your players to catch the ball and throw it accurately. Solid pitching and defense not only win games, they prevent them from being lost.

Throughout this chapter I am going to show you how to teach every player, no matter what his or her ability, to throw a ball accurately. Coaches say to me, "We have 12–15 kids at practice. We don't have time to work with each kid on throwing the baseball." Yes you do, and I am going to demonstrate how you can do it by structuring your practices better and utilizing various drills. The chapter will present a six-step drill, based on the key segments of the throwing motion.

No matter what the players' level, playing catch seems to be a skill coaches overlook. You can count on kids showing up early and looking for baseballs to throw. When the players do start throwing, the activity might appear like playing fetch rather than playing catch. As an experiment, hide the baseballs before practice. The kids will go nuts and start throwing their gloves. Go to a high school baseball first practice. If you are indoors, close your eyes and listen to the banging of the bleachers and the smacking of the wall. You won't have to condition the players at the end of practice. They will get in enough running just playing

Catch Not Fetch

This symbol indicates reference to Companion DVD for Video instruction

fetch. The bottom line: kids cannot instinctively play catch. It must be taught!

Why do you play catch? Most people would tell you that we play catch to loosen our arms. But you got your arm nice and loose in Chapter 2 by stretching your arm with the rotator cuff exercises. We don't play catch to loosen our arms. We play catch to work on throwing the baseball accurately.

Grip The way a person holds the baseball makes all the difference in throwing a ball accurately or not. Changing the grip on the ball can improve almost any player.

 *See Section 3.1*

Four Seams vs. Two Seams

Figure 3.1 *Four seam grip.*

A baseball is constructed with a simple pattern of red stitches for reasons other than keeping the ball intact. Due to aerodynamics, the seams have an impact on the movement of the ball when thrown.

Holding a baseball with a four-seam grip will produce a straight trajectory when at the same time the ball is thrown over the top.

Figure 3.2 *Two seam grip.*

Gripping the ball with four seams means the fingers are held *across* the horseshoe part of the ball. *Note:* the fingers are placed at right angles to the seams. In the four-seam grip the fingers are *not* held parallel to the seams. Thrown with this grip, the ball produces a spinning motion that exposes four seams as it rotates. If you were looking at a ball in slow motion, you would see each of the four seams as the ball turns. On the other hand, have you ever been playing catch and your partner threw a ball that took off to the left or right? Chances are your partner was not holding the ball with four seams. Not using the four-seam grip after fielding a ball can produce an errant throw, which can be costly to a team. Four-seamed grips are imperative if you are going to throw the ball accurately.

Two-seamed grips, on the other hand, are used by pitchers to create movement to fool batters. This grip usually is held with the two seams running side-by-side on the baseball and exposes two seams when rotation occurs. In the two-seam grip the fingers are lined up next to (or parallel with) the seams, and may even be resting over the seams. This grip should not be used to play catch or thrown by fielders. It is a grip for pitchers.

 *See Section 3.2*

Teaching Tip

You don't have time to look down and grab four seams after fielding a ball. A good way to practice getting a four-seam grip without looking is by keeping a ball by your bed at night and practice flipping it into the air, catching it, and rotating it to get a four-seam grip without thinking. It soon becomes instinctual and your fingers "read" the seams like Braille. The result will be that rotating the ball into the proper four-seam grip becomes automatic.

 *See Section 3.3*

Finger (and Thumb) Placement

Once you have the four-seam grip, finger-pressure and placement become important in the throwing process. Whenever you grip the baseball, make sure you hold the ball with a loose grip. Tell a player to throw the ball hard. She will do two things: speed up her throwing motion and grip the ball until the knuckles turn white. Gripping the ball with a tight grip restricts the ball from leaving the hand. Let's conduct an experiment with a slow runner and a fast runner. When the two are in their starting position, hold the faster runner with your hands as he or she tries to accelerate. This holding is similar to the "death grip" on the baseball many players have. When a ball gripped too hard leaves the hand, friction prevents the ball from accelerating at top velocity and may even deter it from finding its target. Tell kids you want to see a gap between the ball and their fingers.

There are times when three fingers are allowable. Usually, in this case, the player's hand is too small to grip the ball with two fingers.

The farther you spread your fingers apart, the slower the ball will travel. Think of your fingers as starting blocks. Spreading your fingers produces separate "starting blocks" from which ball takes off. The closer the "blocks" (fingers closer), the faster the ball will travel.

Finally, a major cause of throwing errors is the thumb. Notice where the thumb is positioned on the baseball. The thumb should be directly underneath the baseball and below the two fingers on top. A lot of kids grip the ball with the thumb to the side, which creates an unstable and off-center resting place from which to launch the ball. The analogy can be made to a bow rest in archery. A firm and correctly positioned rest is needed as the launch pad for the arrow. The rest must be lined up directly under the arrow for it to travel straight. Take the rest and move it to the side a little and see what happens (on second thought, don't try this and take my word for it . . . it could get dangerous).

How many of you were ever taught how to play catch properly? When I speak to coaches at seminars, the first two hours are usually spent on taking care of your arm and playing catch. Coaches then ask, "If you could spend time on only one skill at practice, which one would be the most important?" My answer (playing catch and throwing for accuracy) surprises them.

Playing Catch

If you can help your players throw the baseball accurately, they will win games. Most youth league games are lost by walks and throwing errors. Go to a game tonight and keep track. Usually the team with the fewer throwing errors and least number of walks wins. With that in mind, teaching your players to play catch and hit their target becomes an important part of practice.

Setting Up

See Section 3.4

The first step in teaching kids to play catch is to spread the players apart at a short distance—approximately 10–15 feet. Before a ball is thrown, the player receiving it should give a target. The target should be the glove in the area of the chest. Remember, we are not throwing to loosen up our arms. We are learning to throw for accuracy.

The glove near the chest does two things. First, it offers a target and lets the other person know it is okay to throw. The glove is a signal you are ready to receive the ball. Almost every spring, you will hear someone yell, "Heads up!" because their partner is not paying attention. Giving your partner a target helps eliminate throwing accidents.

Second, a glove gives a small target to aim for. What do you aim for when playing catch? Your focus is probably the other player. If you miss the target (your partner), you may start playing fetch. On the other hand, when your partner gives you a target with the glove, it is no problem if you miss it by a little. The ball will still be close enough to be caught, and chasing balls becomes a thing of the past. In the movie *The Patriot*, when he and his boys are about to ambush the British soldiers, Mel Gibson's character gives advice that has merit for playing catch. He tells his boys, "Aim small, miss small." If I am an archer aiming only at the target as a whole and miss, the arrow may miss the target completely. If I aim for the bulls-eye and miss, the chances are good the arrow will land somewhere on the target. Remind your players to aim small—miss small.

See Section 3.5

Starter Step

Getting the feet in the right position is important for throwing accurately. The first step in "playing catch" is appropriately called the *starter step*. To throw a ball, we need to get a little momentum toward our target and set ourselves up for the next steps. Hence, the *starter step*. Facing your partner, you want to take your first step with the foot on your throwing hand side. For example, if you are right handed you would step with your right foot and vice versa for left-handers. THIS IS NOT PITCHING! Many kids play catch by going straight into a windup. You need to reinforce the point that all throwing is not pitching, and the first step

Figure 3.3 *Starter step.*

needs to be with the toe pointed toward their target or a little to the right of their target. How many times does a player field a ball as an infielder or outfielder and go into a windup? The starter step will get your momentum going to your target and will reduce stress on the arm. The step should not be gigantic. It should be a normal, controlled step that enables you to push off with your back foot. Taking this step also lines up the player's body for the next step in the throwing process.

Lining Up Your Scope

See Section 3.6

Figure 3.4 *Lining up the scope.*

After taking the starter step, you need to line up your lead shoulder (the shoulder on your glove-side). I call this the *scope*. When we aim a gun at its intended target, we use a scope to accurately pinpoint its location. In this case, your arm is the "gun," and your lead shoulder becomes the gun's "scope," which points toward the ball's target. Calling it a "lead shoulder" is dull and drab for kids and is thus ineffective. Terming the shoulder a "scope" is cool, and the kids latch on immediately. The opposite leg from the "starter step" leg should swing around and be lined up with the receiving partner. It will help bring your "scope" into the correct throwing position.

Teaching Tip

When discussing complex baseball terms with kids, make sure to rename certain skills into "kid lingo." Not only will the kids now understand what you are saying to them, but it also helps them to remember the skill.

"Thigh, Waving Good-bye"

See Section 3.7

We have received the target from our partner, a good starter step has been taken, and the scope is lined up for an accurate approach. The next step is to throw the ball. The body is in a good, balanced position to perform the task. Right now the hand is in your glove somewhere around the chest area. When you go to throw the ball, the hand and glove separate. At that point, the arm holding the ball should extend toward the ground and graze the thigh. From there the ball should pass the thigh and extend directly behind the player with the palm of the throwing hand facing away. The glove hand should be extended and pointed toward the target.

Figure 3.5 *"Thigh, wave good-bye."*

Try explaining all these steps to a young player! This is where "kid lingo" comes in handy. We say, "Thigh, waving good-bye" or "thigh, high-five." With this catchy mnemonic, kids learn a lot quicker and start processing immediately. We also call this motion "the long C." The motion of grazing your thigh (and I actually brush my thigh and make a sound to help teach it) and waving goodbye produces an arc that resembles a big '"C." Right now you are 3/4 of the way around that "C." Why a "long C"? A "short C" produces a lot of pressure on the elbow and does not utilize the shoulder as much. Consequently, most kids who throw with a "short C" have elbow problems. There are times players should throw with a "short C." These situations will be discussed in chapters 7, 8, and 9 on fielding.

 *See Section 3.8*

Arm Slots

Now that we are lined up, let's actually throw the ball to our partner. From the "thigh, waving good-bye" position, your glove hand should tuck in or pull as you drive with your backside toward your target. The throwing arm comes through and should be in the "L position" as it passes your head. Your arm slot dictates whether the ball is going to go high or low. The term "arm slot" refers to the position of the arm when the ball leaves the pitcher's hand. The trajectory of the throw is dependent on where and how the arm is positioned, or what "slot" it is in. Releasing the ball too soon results in a high throw. Here "soon" means a point where the arm is still behind the head. In this arm slot, the hand may be facing up. If you release the ball after the arm passes the head, or "late," the resulting throw will sail low. To learn how to control a throw, experimenting with various arm slots can be helpful. Once a player understands his or her arm slots, control of the ball high and low becomes easier. The lead elbow controls the direction of the ball left or right. Here it's helpful to think of darts. The lead elbow is very important in throwing a dart accurately to the target. As your arm comes by the head in the "L position," it should extend past the head and end up with the lead elbow pointed at the target. This will produce consistency in throwing and allow you to hit your target more often. With the lead elbow lined up and your body in a balanced, powerful position, the correct arm slot will result in an on-target throw.

Follow-through

 *See Section 3.9*

The important thing with the follow-through is not to stop your momentum after releasing the ball. After the ball is released, the arm should extend across the knee opposite the throwing arm. The back leg should come through, and you should end up in a good fielding position.

Teaching Tip

There is a teaching tool to help reinforce the follow-through motion. Have the players sweep the grass with the throwing hand after releasing the ball. Once the ball is thrown, the player should continue the arm motion until the fingers graze the grass. This exaggerated gesture helps reinforce the follow-through.

Knockout

 See Section 3.10

There are many different games to help players work on throwing accurately. The best game, considering time constraints and effectiveness, is knockout.

Knockout combines playing catch and focusing on hitting a target. The object of the game is to throw the ball and hit your opponent in the chest (not literally!). If you hit your opponent in the chest, you receive one point. Your opponent, or partner, then returns a throw and tries to hit you in the chest. Each player continues to give a glove target. The game can be played to a predetermined point total. I would keep it around five points to start. Remember to stress that the shoulders and waist are target areas different from the chest.

A variant of this game is to award points for hitting the head. I do not recommend this, especially for young players. Many young kids are already scared of the baseball, and trying to catch the ball at face-level generally doesn't lead to learning a skill.

Fixing Throwing Mechanics

It is not enough to tell you what every player should be doing right. You are probably saying, "Okay, I understand what each player should be doing, but how do I change their motions?" It is a difficult task to fix mechanics while players are throwing at full-speed. I have seen coaches trying to do this, and it's hard for even the well-trained eye. Each segment of the throwing motion must be isolated to diagnose a problem. Slowing the motion down, breaking it into parts, and working on specific drills can help you correct almost any throwing flaw.

It is important to note that the following drills isolate skills that build on one another. The later steps incorporate proper performance of the earlier ones. If all six steps are done correctly and in sequence, an error-free throwing motion will result. Repetition of the steps in order will help make the motion a habit.

Six-step Isolation Drill for Throwing Mechanics

Isolation drills can be done individually or as a team. Players will need to have a partner. The drills are supposed to be done together. But, once a problem is diagnosed, the specific drill that addresses the problem can be done for a time exclusively. Every ball thrown in these drills should be caught at the center of the chest, which is targeted with the glove. If the ball lands either to the left or right of the chest, a mechanical flaw is exposed. Every ball should be in line vertically with the head and should be caught squarely in the middle of the chest. Stress the importance of accuracy and not velocity. Players want to impress you with their arm strength. Remind them that accuracy is more important than velocity.

Step 1: The Wrist-flick

 See Section 3.11

Figure 3.6 *The wrist-flick.*

Two players should be approximately four feet apart for the wrist-flick drill. The person delivering the ball should hold his glove out in front of the body and place the throwing arm elbow in the glove. The reason for the elbow in the glove is so the player isolates the throwing arm. It is important that the elbow and forearm do not move in this drill. The drill focuses on the wrist only. In this drill, you want to observe the player gripping the baseball with a four-seamed grip, with space between the finger and ball, and the ball leaving the player's hand with backward rotation. The player receiving the ball should be giving a target in the center of his or her chest. Make sure the thumb is directly under the ball. Give a backward, then forward, flick of the wrist to deliver the ball. The skill should then be repeated by the thrower's partner. The wrist-flick is great for observing mechanical flaws with the grip and for focusing on the ball as it leaves the player's hand.

Step 2: The Forearm Toss

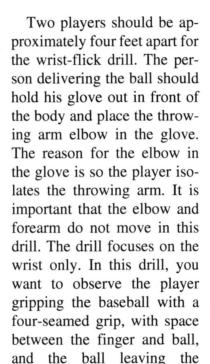 *See Section 3.12*

In the forearm toss drill, the throwing partners should be approximately six feet apart. The setup is similar to the wrist-flick drill, with the glove held in front and the throwing elbow in the glove. This time, however, the forearm is used. The forearm comes back and then moves forward, like the motion of a catapult. Stress that the rest of the body stays quiet and does not move. Players will want to move their shoulders or glove to help them throw the ball. The forearm comes back, and then goes forward—with the wrist-flick in step one also being used. Look for the player's wrist and forearm falling off to the left or right during this drill. Movement to the left or right will produce an inaccurate throw. The forearm and wrist both need to come straight back and then go forward to induce a precise throw.

 *See Section 3.13*

Step 3: Shooting Darts

An 8–10-foot distance between the players should be used for the shooting darts drill. The players should be sitting on the ground facing one another, with their legs spread apart in a comfortable "V" position. The legs are taken away during this drill. With the throwing elbow lined up directly towards a partner, the thrower should deliver the ball with a dart-throwing motion. Many times kids want to push the elbow off to the side because it feels comfortable. The elbow serves as a guide to line up the ball with the target. Watch for the elbow flaring out to the side. Lining up the elbow will feel uncomfortable at first, but the results will prove effective. The ball should land, once again, at the chest and vertically in line with the head.

 *See Section 3.14*

Step 4: One-knee Drill

Each player should be kneeling on one (their throwing-side) knee and be spaced 15–20 feet apart from a partner. While resting the throwing-side knee on the ground, the opposite leg should be up with the toe pointing at the target. It is important to keep the torso upright and "standing tall" for the one-knee drill. The glove and ball (both hands) should be in front of the body facing the partner, or over the toe facing the partner. For this drill, the player rotates the torso with the throwing arm going "thigh, waving good-bye" and subsequently lines up the lead shoulder, or "scope." The ball is delivered to the partner, who should remain in the same position giving a target with his or her glove. Remember, this drill and its motion should include the three previous steps.

Figure 3.7 *One-knee drill.*

The elbow leads towards the target, and the wrist and forearm should produce a catapult action with the ball, when released, rotating backwards from the four-seam grip. It is important in this drill after release of the ball to follow through across the front knee. Again, missing right or left of the target indicates a mechanical flaw in the throwing motion. Watch for players not generating a "long C" or failing to line up their "scope."

Step 5: No-stride Toss (Power Position)

 See Section 3.15

Partners should be about 25 feet apart for the no-stride toss. The drill is great for teaching pitchers to use their legs while throwing. Pitching will be discussed in chapters 10 and 11. For the no-stride toss, the players should already have their legs spread apart. This position is similar to that of a pitcher who's already taken his or her stride from the mound. Kids sometimes get too extended and don't use their legs when throwing the baseball. Stand beside a player and mark where the glove-side foot lands. After marking it, have him or her put a foot in the mark and throw the ball from that spot using their legs. Finding out how little (or much) the legs are used is important in the learning process.

The no-stride drill helps players utilize their legs when throwing. Make sure the legs are spread apart in a good, balanced position. The distance is similar to a three-point stance in football, or a batter's position after already taking a stride. The "scope" is lined up and the thrower is standing in a position comparable to a pitcher's position in the stretch. With both hands out in front, the thrower should load up on the back side. The "back side" refers to rocking back on the back leg similar to a boxer about to deliver a powerful punch. It is important that the head does not go past the back leg. Such a position is referred to as "overloading." The player should then deliver the ball, incorporating all of the other steps learned previously.

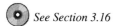 *See Section 3.16*

Step 6: Normal Throwing Position

Now that we've isolated the throwing motion into its key segments, it's time to assemble them into one fluid motion. Take the starter step to your target and deliver the ball to the chest area of your partner. The mechanics should all come together harmoniously. Refer back to the "playing catch" portion of this chapter for more detail on the starter step.

 *See Section 3.17*

Long Toss

A great way to strengthen your arm is to long toss regularly. Long toss refers to the throwing of a ball or playing catch at a farther distance than normal. Teaching the arm to go beyond its customary limits is important in the strengthening process. There are, however, detrimental consequences if this is done incorrectly. You should be conscious of safety and avoid over-exertion with the long toss.

When long tossing, make sure to start at a short distance (10 feet). Starting the long toss at a great distance is a mistake. The arm must first get loose. Only when it does, should you slowly work your way back to a greater distance with each throw you make.

Another controversial long-toss topic is throwing with or without an arc on the ball. Allow your players to throw with an arc if they need to. In order to really stretch the arm out, it is necessary to throw with an arc. When you move to a shorter distance after long-tossing, your throws might be higher than normal. Snapping the ball down with the throwing arm and following through can be emphasized. and learning can take place. Snapping the ball down adds velocity and keeps the ball at a lower height.

Make sure players are using good mechanics when throwing at a longer than usual distance. The mechanics should be fluid, and the motion unhurried. The ball should not be off-line to the left or right when long-tossing. If the ball doesn't reach the target, that is okay. You are trying to stretch the arm out and throw a long distance. Correct the same bad habits in the long toss as you would do in "regular" catch.

Lastly, throw for a reasonable amount of time. The amount of time depends on the person throwing. There is no standard time you should devote to long-tossing. The throwing motion is the fastest movement the human body can make. The arm will get tired, and mechanics will start breaking down if the players don't move closer. You should always end long-tossing by having the players move closer. The arm can become slightly inflamed, and you want to cool the arm down by moving to a closer, more comfortable distance. Icing the arm should be done to help minimize inflammation.

Summary

Many coaches and players believe working on throwing is a waste of time. Everyone knows how to throw a ball! While throwing a ball can be performed by anyone with an able arm, throwing with accuracy and good mechanics consistently is a lost art. Teaching players to throw accurately is a valuable and necessary skill. It ranks #1 on my list of basic baseball skills.

CHAPTER 4

Hitting

"Hitting is the most important part of the game. It is where the big money is, where much of the status is, and the fan interest."
—Ted Williams

ORMER Dodgers' manager Tommy Lasorda once said, "My theory of hitting was just to watch the ball as it came in and hit it." While Mr. Lasorda's approach to hitting seems simple, hitting a baseball is possibly the hardest skill to do in any sport. In order to be a great hitter, you need flawless mechanics and impeccable timing. How do you teach these to a young player?

Learning to hit at a young age is important. A boy or girl learning baseball is like a fresh piece of clay: pliable, impressionable, and unburdened by motor muscle memory. As the clay is used over time, it becomes harder and is not as easy to mold into a desirable form. The older a player is, the harder it is to change his or her bad habits. When a player's young, it is easier to develop sound fundamentals.

There is no magic formula for building the perfect hitting specimen. Several basics, however, are common to all good hitters. While other publications speak at a high level arguing the finer points of hitting, this book will expose you to the undisputed skills you need to hit a baseball well. These skills break down into four phases of hitting, supplemented with intangibles that will have an effect on your approach at the plate. Subsequent chapters provide drills and techniques for correcting hitters' flaws.

This symbol indicates reference to Companion DVD for video instruction

On-deck/Mental Approach

Ted Williams once said, "Hitting is fifty percent above the shoulders." Some would argue that it is closer to ninety percent. If so much depends on the mind, then a person can have a great fundamental swing and still not be a very good hitter. Even before you can improve the physical parts of hitting, you have to exercise the muscle between the ears.

The first thing you can create is a positive attitude. This advice is also a good starting point for life in general. Too many players come to the plate with a defeatist attitude. Instead of saying, "I am going to mash the ball. I am going to win this battle and get a base hit," the player is thinking, "Oh, please let me hit the ball. This guy throws hard and I hope I don't embarrass myself." Tell your players what they say to themselves "inside" is important. It's always good to say to themselves: "I can do it." Taking a deep breath can help. Players can also get their mind on hitting by focusing on the pitcher—more specifically on how and what the pitcher is throwing. If the situation wasn't hard enough, now we fill the stands with people. It becomes a pressure-filled time full of emotion at the plate. Make sure everyone, including coaches and parents, are displaying focus with their actions as well as their words.

There is a lot of time in the dugout between at-bats. This is a valuable time to study the pitcher. What does he throw to everyone on the first pitch? When the pitcher gets ahead of the hitter, does she have a tendency to throw a certain pitch? Is there something in the pitcher's delivery that gives away pitches to the hitter? These are all observations that can be made by the players in the dugout during a game. Studying the tendencies of your pitching opponent can help you stay ahead of the competition and have a positive influence on your next at-bat.

Second, think about what's happening in the game before you step up to the plate. Knowing what you need to do at the plate for the team to be successful will help you become a better player (and help your team win games). A player should be aware that hitting is more than just batting a ball. Good hitting is an attempt to put the ball in play in a way that will lead to runs. If there's a player on third with less than one out, a fly ball to the outfield should be the hitter's goal. Look for a pitch up in the strike zone to lift to the outfield. If you need to move the runner from second to third, hit the ball to the right side of the field. A high school baseball coach recently complained to me how his freshman players came to him not understanding the game. When a player goes to the plate, she should think about the situation and what needs to be done to help the team score the run. Coaches will always find a place in the starting line-up for players who execute fundamental team hitting.

Lastly, look for one pitch early in the count. Coaches who make their players take the first pitch are taking the bat out of a kid's hands. It's true that at times taking a pitch may be a beneficial tactic. Examples are when the pitcher is having trouble throwing strikes, your team is behind by a lot of runs and needs base-runners, or maybe you want to give a runner on base a chance to steal. If none of these apply, it is "go-time" when at the plate. Ask a kid what his favorite pitch is and have him show you where at the plate he wants it. This becomes the only pitch to swing at until he receives the first strike. I call this "the mashing zone." How many players swing at a ball in the dirt on the first pitch? If the ball is an outside strike and you are looking inside, don't swing. Take it. You have two more swings left. Be confident and less selective for the remaining two strikes. But until you get that first strike, wait for a pitch in "your mashing zone." This creates plate discipline and improves your chances for success.

Teaching Tip

One way to instill plate discipline is during batting practice. One tip I give all hitters is to swing at only strikes when at the plate. Many times coaches have trouble throwing strikes during batting practice. Due to their errant throwing, players swing at any pitch close to the plate to speed up batting practice. There are times the coach encourages the player to swing at anything close. It is important for hitters *not* to swing at bad pitches, even during practice. Practicing not swinging is important. The saying is valid, "Practice how you are going to play."

Phase I: Stance/Pre-flight Check

The stance may be the most important phase of hitting. While all of the other phases of hitting are important, the stance is the starting point. Before a pilot takes off, she checks all the gauges and equipment to make sure the plane is in good working order. Let's face it, there is no good place to pull over and fix the problem in the sky. The same holds true for the batting stance. Before you swing and "launch" your bat through the zone (remember that "L" word . . . it will be revisited in the next segment), you need to make sure everything is in good working order.

See Section 4.1

Where Do I Stand?

Stand in a spot where the entire plate can be covered. Players sometimes move up in the batter's box for a slow pitcher or someone who throws a lot of off-speed pitches, and move back in the box for hard throwers. I do not recommend either of these tactics. Stand in the same spot regardless of the type of pitcher. What is the reason? The pitcher must throw the ball so it crosses the plate between the batter's knees and chest. If you can cover the entire plate with the bat, why move? If the pitcher is throwing hard, you need to load up a little sooner (see phase II for the load-up position). If the pitcher is throwing curves that break low, let them go, because they are balls anyway. Learn not to move your feet. Each person has his or her own strike zone. Learn yours and get used to it. Standing in the same spot in the batter's box will help you learn your strike zone.

Develop a Soft Focus

Vision is important when it comes to hitting. If you don't believe me, blindfold yourself and take a few swings. Vision is, first of all, being able to see as clearly as possible. It is advisable for players to have a regular eye examination. The second thing is develop a *soft focus*. A soft focus occurs when you concentrate on an area where the ball comes out of the pitcher's hand. Usually this is an imaginary box or frame above the pitcher's throwing shoulder. Most people look directly at the pitcher when he is delivering the ball to the plate. When the ball is thrown, you have approximately 0.4 (four tenths) of a second to decide whether to swing. In those precious tenths of a second, a decision needs to be made on the path of the bat, and the timing needs to be accurate. If you do not develop a soft focus, you will see that time is wasted trying to pick the ball up between the moment it leaves the pitcher's hand and when it crosses the plate. This time can be re-captured by focusing on the ball when it leaves the pitcher's hand. The extra one- or two tenths of a second allows the hitter to make a better decision and eliminate guessing.

TV Face

 *See Section 4.2*

Figure 4.1 *TV face.*

Players will often "hide" one of their eyes while in their batting stance. When standing at the plate, their head is tilted to one side, or their face is buried in the front shoulder. Hitting a baseball is tough. Try hitting while using only one eye! I use the term "TV face" when presenting the topic of positioning the eyes. In order to see the ball, players must look at the pitcher using both eyes, as they do when watching television. Go home tonight and try to watch TV with one eye or with your head tilted to one side. It is no picnic. Have kids turn their face to look at the pitcher with both eyes.

Feet

 *See Section 4.3*

The key part of any building is the foundation. With a weak foundation, a house will not be strong, and structural problems will arise. The same holds true for hitting. A solid foundation must

See Section 4.4

Teaching Tip

There is an effective way to get players into a strong athletic stance at the plate. When the player is in his normal stance, take the bat away and ask him to get into a 3-point football stance. With the feet stationary, have the player lift the hand touching the ground and then stand up in an upright position. You have found the optimal stance for that player. The stance will vary somewhat depending on the player's physical build.

---

be established and kept throughout the hitting process. The foundation is the feet. In the stance, the feet should be at least shoulder-width apart. Pick a sport and I will describe for you a good, sound athletic position where the feet are spread at least shoulder-width apart. In many lessons, the first thing that needs to be addressed is the feet.

With the feet in position, the next step is getting the right balance. The weight of your body should be on the balls of your feet. Your feet should be flat, but with the weight shifted toward your toes. Players sometimes want to lift their heels and get on their toes. This is not comfortable and not as strong as keeping the feet relatively flat.

 *See Section 4.5*

Teaching Tip

Tell players to keep their "nose over their toes." With the nose over the toes, it is really hard to be either "flat footed" or on the heels of your feet. Your weight automatically shifts forward, and you will have better balance and power.

Lastly, we need to utilize the strength of the legs. The feet are spread shoulder-width apart, and the weight is on the balls of the feet. Now we need to make sure everything is strong. To do this, bend the knees slightly and turn them inward. If a player can be knocked over from the side, he is not bending the knees correctly. Turning the toes inward just a little will help sometimes too. If the hitter were to walk in this position, he would look bowlegged. This position will help solidify the legs and put the hitter in an optimal position to get the most out of the lower body.

 *See Section 4.6*

Teaching Tip

While in the stance, have the hitter wedge a basketball or volleyball between the legs above the kneecaps. The hitter should perform a squeezing motion to keep the ball from moving. Now, have the hitter take a few swings with the bat off a tee. The ball should stay in the same spot between the legs. This will not only promote a great stance, but will also instill balance in the swing. You might be surprised how well the hitter actually hits the ball doing this drill.

Hands

 *See Section 4.7*

To be a good hitter, it helps to have good hands. Some kids have great hands, and yet still grip or hold a bat poorly.

Teaching Tip

Want more whip action in a player's swing? Have the player get in the stance and swing the bat. This time, however, tell him or her to let the bat fly through the air. Let's see how far the bat can be thrown. The kid will first look at you like you are crazy. Not only is this drill fun for the players, but it teaches them to throw or whip the bat through the zone and let it fly. With a tight grip, the bat won't fly far. When doing this drill it is important that all other players stand at a good distance behind the player throwing the bat. In fact, it is best if all players are behind a backstop.

 *See Section 4.8*

The first thing a hitter must do is grip the bat *lightly*. Too many players think that the tighter their grip on the bat, the farther the ball will go. They tighten up their muscles and swing as hard as they can. The opposite is the case. In order to swing the bat fast, a loose grip needs to be applied. Pine tar was invented to allow such a grip. Mention to your players that huge and muscular big leaguers occasionally lose their bats when they swing because they are applying a loose grip. One way to remind players of how to hold the bat is the slogan: "Loose grip, more whip."

The second thing you need to do is line up your knocking knuckles. You have two sets of knuckles: "the punching knuckles" and "the knocking knuckles." In order to get the

Figure 4.2 *Aligning the knocking knuckles.*

 *See Section 4.9*

quick whip needed, the knocking knuckles on both hands must be lined up (or be very close). This grip is used so the bat can smoothly and quickly move through the zone. With the knocking knuckles aligned, the hands and wrists experience a free-flowing motion.

Teaching Tip

There is an easy way to teach the concept of aligning the knuckles. Put the bat between your feet with the tip of the barrel on the ground. Reach down with your hands and grip the bat like you are going to swing it. Lift the bat up, and you have your knocking knuckles lined up (see Figure 4.2).

Lastly, the hands should be holding the bat near the back shoulder, which is the shoulder farther from the pitcher. If you're a right-handed hitter, this would be the right shoulder. The exact location is not important, but having the hands in the area of the back shoulder is imperative in order to get to the next phase correctly. You do not want your hands too high, too low, or too far back behind your back shoulder. This will be explained in more detail when Phase II of the swing is discussed.

 *See Section 4.10*

Elbows

The number one myth in hitting is get the back elbow up. Go to just about any youth baseball game in America and inevitably you'll hear the shout, "Get your back elbow up!" I'm here to tell you that this concept is wrong! Since I was old enough to swing a bat, I can remember the five words (Get Your Back Elbow Up). They are like an heirloom passed down from generation to generation.

Why do people think the back elbow should be up? Many kids drop their back elbow when they swing, or "loop" to the ball. The fix, apparently, is to raise the back elbow in the stance, so that it doesn't "drop" during the swing. Unfortunately, the elbow must come back on the same path, and inevitably you'll drop it even farther. Not to get too technical, here's why. Many of us have heard Newton's third law of motion, which states "For every action there is an equal and opposite reaction." When you drop your back elbow, the front shoulder must come up. The back elbow ris-

Figure 4.3a *Back elbow up.*   **Figure 4.3b** *Elbows pointed down (spaghetti arms).*

ing higher leads to an even more pronounced loop in the swing. I equate telling a player to get the back elbow up to mishandling a situation with someone that has a chocolate addiction. To prevent a person from eating chocolate, the solution would not be to send the addict to the Hershey Chocolate factory and hang out in the taste-testing room. If you are dropping your back elbow, why would you prescribe raising it even more? When the bat is swung, the drop is going to be even bigger. The situation has only been made worse! The back elbow should be down in the stance. Both elbows should dangle like two pieces of cooked spaghetti. Help your players remember to keep the arms loose by mentioning "spaghetti arms." The elbows should be relaxed and pointing towards the ground. The back elbow, when raised, produces a slower bat. The elbow has to travel farther to get the hands through the zone. In Phase II, we will discuss where the elbows are positioned.

Movement

See Section 4.11

The hitter must have rhythm while standing at the plate. Players who stand motionless in the batter's box are putting themselves at a disadvantage. It is more difficult (that is, more work) to accelerate from a state of rest than from a state motion. Let's conduct an experiment. We will race, but I will begin moving from a position behind you. When I reach your starting point, you can take off. With my head start, I am willing to bet I'll be ahead of you for the first few yards. While standing at the plate, movement not only gives the hitter a head start, it also allows the body to stay loose. The more tense hitters are, the slower their muscles become. These factors point to the conclusion that a hitter should engage in some small movement or motion while standing at the plate. Mike Schmidt used to have a little bit of a waggle. Derek Jeter and Albert Pujols have a signature movement with their arms and front leg. Motion is important in the stance.

With all of that said, too much movement becomes a problem. The motion we are discussing is small and controlled. Too much unnecessary movement of the body can create movement of the eyes or create flaws in the swing. More movement = more problems. What is too much movement? It is movement that impairs your ability to get to Phase II of the hitting process. There is a fine line between too little or too much movement, and this needs to be determined by the hitter and the coach.

Bottom Line

The batter's stance must be comfortable and balanced. Vision must be 100%, the body and hands need to be loose, and the base (the feet) must be powerfully balanced. With all of these things in place, you are ready to move on to Phase II of the hitting process.

Phase II: The Launch Position (loading up)

See Section 4.12

Let's talk boxing. To deliver a powerful punch, a boxer must pull the arm back so that it can move forward with maximum power. If the arm doesn't go back, the punch is simply a weak jab. The same holds true for hitting. In both sports, the stances are fairly similar—with boxers having a more open stance at times. Boxers hold their hands as hitters do. Of course, in their way, boxers are hitters. In baseball, swinging the bat with power and speed requires taking the hands back or recoiling a little to produce a hard, fast swing.

See Section 4.13

Stride

Part of the loading-up process involves taking a stride. The

Figure 4.4 *Stride.*

stride should be short and soft, as though you are stepping on an egg carton. The length of the stride relates to the timing of when the swing starts. A long stride increases movement, which in turn means committing sooner to the swing. A short stride is easier, since the legs will be shoulder-width apart, or a little more. A short stride also allows the hitter more time to make a decision to swing.

When the stride foot lands, the leg straightens and the foot should be closed. A closed foot is one that has the toes pointing toward home plate. An opened foot is one where the batter points the toes toward the pitcher when the stride-foot lands. Opening the front foot leads to problems in the swing phase. Players who pull their front shoulder or let the front side fly open too fast usually open their lead foot. Opening the front foot puts the front shoulder in motion, and as a result the hips open prematurely. How do you teach a player not to pull his or her front shoulder? One way is to have the player practice keeping the front foot closed until after the swing.

Why does the front leg straighten? The front leg straightens so the hitter's weight stays back and the hips can generate more power. If the front leg does not straighten, chances are the weight is shifting too soon onto the front foot and a lot of power is lost. The stiff front leg serves as a prop to channel all of the energy and explosiveness from the hips to the point of contact.

Hands

See Section 4.14

At the same time the stride is taken, the hands need to go back. In the stance, the optimal position for the hands is in the area of the back shoulder. From this position, the hands should go back a couple of inches. The lead arm, or the arm facing the pitcher, should not straighten. This straightening of the arm produces a "front arm bar." A front arm bar produces a slower swing and creates other problems in Phase III of the hitting process.

When the hands go back, be sure the barrel of the bat does not wrap behind the head. We call this "bat wrap." When the hands go back, the barrel should go back, too. It takes a lot more time to get the barrel to the hitting zone when it is positioned behind the head. The swing is much quicker when the barrel is not wrapped around the head.

Figure 4.5 *Hands back.*

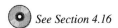 *See Section 4.15*

Movement

It is important that the stride goes forward and the hands go back, or recoil, at the same time. If both stride and recoil are done together, the head will remain stationary. Think of a balance scale or a see-saw. When you shift weight to one side, the opposite side

See Section 4.16

Teaching Tip

When working on loading up and keeping the head still, place a bobber or some small object on the end of fishing line and hang it from the ceiling. The bobber should be at nose-level. Practice taking the stride and recoiling with the hands, and start with the bobber even with your nose. After loading up, check the bobber to make sure your weight is distributed properly and the bobber ends up in line with your nose or head. Moving too far in front of or behind the bobber means too much head movement.

---

must be counterbalanced. It is important your weight goes back, and it is also critical that your head stays stationary. This will put you in a good launch position. The head staying stationary allows the hitter to see the ball with fixed eyes as opposed to moving ones. Try to read a book while moving back and forth. It is much easier to read—and bat—when the head is kept still.

Now that everything is in order before the ball arrives, it is "go-time," the time to swing. The previous two phases of hitting will get you in a good position to hit the ball. The swing, however, is the crucial part of the hitting process. Phases I and II won't matter, unless you execute a good swing, which also makes solid contact with the ball.

Phase III: The Swing

Choosing a Bat

What size bat should a player use? The answer is simple. Look at the player holding and swinging the bat. Does it look too big in her hands when she swings it? Then it is too big. Does it look too small? Then it is too small. As long as a player is able to swing a bat with speed and control, that bat can be right for that hitter. With the ounce-to-length ratio of bats on the market today, the rules have been thrown out the window in regard to the size of the bat a player uses. A ball struck by a larger and heavier bat will travel farther. The more mass (heavier the bat) you can swing hard (quick swing), the farther the struck ball will go. Again, the key assumption with bat selection is being certain the player can swing the bat properly, which requires asking the player, as well as observing her.

Contact Points

 See Section 4.17

Contact points are key places where you should make contact with the baseball depending on where it crosses the plate. The contact point will differ depending on where the pitch is.

Inside Pitch

The inside pitch should be hit in front of the plate a couple of inches. This obviously depends on the size of the hitter and the length of bat he or she is using.

Down the Middle

The pitch down the middle should be hit right in front of the plate and driven up the middle.

Outside Pitch

The outside pitch should be hit back on the plate and driven to the opposite field. Many players try to pull this ball, resulting in a weak grounder to the left side or a pop-up. "Pulling a ball" refers to hitting a ball to the same side of the field in which the batter is standing in the batter's box. If the hitter is left-handed, this would be to right field (a right-handed hitter would hit the ball to left field). It takes discipline to wait for the outside pitch and drive it to the opposite field.

 *See Section 4.18*

Long Swing vs. Short Swing

For a hitter to be successful at any level, a short swing must be learned. Barry Bonds has one of the shortest, most compact swings in the game. He rarely gets beat on the inner part of the plate because he is so fast getting the barrel of the bat to the ball.

A short swing is when the hitter takes his hands directly to the ball and gets his bat through the zone using the quickest possible route. The elbows never extend until just at contact or directly after contact.

A long swing, on the other hand, is when the hitter gets his arms extended away from his body too early and usually executes a "front arm bar," which was defined above in discussing the launch position. Instead of taking the hands directly to the ball, the hands extend out away from the body, and the swing takes a longer route to the ball. The elbows straighten earlier and power is lost. Practice throwing punches with the arms extended too early. Lock the elbows and restrict them from bending. The punches will lose their power and have no effect on the opponent. This correlates to hitting with a long swing.

Teaching Tip

Swinging with bent elbows to produce a short, fast swing is important. This does not mean the elbows should be tucked in toward the body. Many players will tuck the elbows inward and lose a lot of power. The hands and elbows are thrown forward and should never be in contact with the body. The player should get full extension upon contact with the ball.

Level Swing vs. Chopping Wood   *See Section 4.19*

One of the more heated debates in hitting involves the swing's trajectory. The bone of contention is between "chopping wood" (swinging down on the ball) and taking a level swing. My recommendation is that both have relevance. Draw a triangle from your hands (point A) to approximately eight inches below your hands (point B) to where you want to make contact with the ball (point C). This triangle is visualized while you are in your stance. The shortest distance between two points is a straight line. So, taking that rule of geometry into account, you should take the hands from point A to point C. In fact, doing so creates a downward angle during the swing.

Right before impact, however, the bat should be leveled slightly to hit the baseball. Most "chopping wood" theorists believe that swinging down on the ball produces backspin. Swinging down also produces a lot of ground balls.

Here's an experiment. Imagine the pitched ball is a nail, and the bat is a hammer. The pitcher is slightly raised, since he is throwing from a mound. When he delivers the ball, which is compared to a nail traveling head first, the head will be moving at a slightly downward angle. What about the hammer (the bat)? If the nail is traveling toward the plate at a slightly downward angle (head first), where do you want to swing the hammer to hit the nail? Common sense would say at a slightly upward angle. How, then, do you produce backspin on the baseball? Hit the bottom half of the baseball. As you can see, a good swing involves a downward approach, level swing, and slight uppercut. All three, in conjunction with one another, will produce a good swing.

See Section 4.20

Palm Up/Palm Down

When contact is made, the wrists should not roll over. That the wrists need to be rolled over while swinging is a baseball myth. The wrists are definitely used when swinging the bat, but they do not roll over until *after* contact. On contact, the top hand should be palm up, and the bottom hand should be palm down. The palm up/palm down position is much more powerful than rolling over the wrists.

Figure 4.6 *Palm up/palm down.*

See Section 4.21

Whipping the Bat

As mentioned in the pre-flight check when discussing the hands, the bat should be gripped lightly and whipped through the zone. Gripping the bat tightly does inhibit bat speed.

Teaching Tip

With a player in the batting stance, position the bat at the point it makes contact with the ball. Have the player first roll the wrists over. Push against the bat and have the player resist the pushing as if they are swinging through you. After doing this, have them do the same thing using a palm up/palm down approach. The variation in strength is quite noticeable, and players will quickly see and feel the difference between the two positions.

See Section 4.22

Squish the Bug

Using the hips for power and explosiveness is important in hitting a ball with force. To engage the hips, the back foot must pivot so the hips can clear and allow the bat to travel through the zone. This is referred to as "squishing the bug." The player should visualize a bug under the back foot and squish it as the swing is performed. There is such a thing as "over-squishing" the bug. If you rotate too far, balance will be lost and so will power. When squishing the bug, the back leg should finish in an "L" position. The front leg stays straight, while the back leg forms an "L". The body should stay upright, with the back leg driving from a bending position. Squishing the bug and forming the "L" can be practiced anywhere.

The follow-through refers to the completion of your swing after making contact with the baseball. Without a good follow-through, hitters will have trouble swinging with power and making solid contact.

Phase IV: The Follow-through

Finishing the Swing

 *See Section 4.23*

After making contact with the ball, the hitter should continue the swing until some other force stops the bat's momentum. In other words, swing through the baseball and don't stop the swing after impact. Let the bat travel through the ball and finish somewhere behind the body. People argue about whether hitters should follow through high or low with the bat. It makes no difference. Mike Schmidt followed through low. On the other hand, Ken Griffey follows through high. The location of the finish doesn't matter, as long as you are swinging through the baseball and letting the bat continue its path until it stops somewhere behind you.

Hand Release vs. No Hand Release

 *See Section 4.24*

There is no advantage in letting go of the top hand after the swing. Charlie Lau, a former major league hitting instructor, was an influential huge proponent of releasing the top hand after the swing. His theory was that it ensured complete extension through the ball. It also allows the shoulders and head to stay down on the ball easier and keeps the "nose over the toes." Unfortunately, parents and players see major league hitters letting go of the bat and try to adopt the approach on their own. This can lead to a bad habit. Instead of letting go of the bat well after contact, the player lets go of the bat at contact and thus hits the ball with one hand. It is true that certain major league hitters do let go of their top hand. However, they do so well after contact to get more extension. When we see it at full speed on TV, it looks as though the hitter is letting go of the bat at contact. On the other hand, if you were to replay the swing in slow motion, you would be able to see the hitter letting go of the top hand after contact to get the extension. Whether you want to let go of the bat or not is a personal decision. My advice is to keep both hands on the bat. If a player releases the top hand correctly, don't change this movement. But, if there is a premature release of the hand, make sure to teach using both hands when swinging the bat.

 *See Section 4.25*

Head Position

After making contact with the ball, hitters can develop a bad habit of raising their head to see where the ball goes. This "looking up" occurs before the swing is finished and the follow-through complete. Pulling the head (and inevitably the shoulder with the head) creates the problem of pulling the hands away from the plate. Develop the habit of keeping the head down until after

Figure 4.7 *Head position.*   **Figure 4.8** *Hand release.*

contact is made with the ball. This can be practiced and reinforced by doing hitting drills properly. When swinging during a drill, exaggerate keeping the head down.

Teaching Tip

The best training device for fixing the "looking up" problem is the batting tee. After contact is made with the ball, the player's head should stay down and the eyes remain focused on the tee. The ball should not be followed, and a net should be used to eliminate the ball from traveling anywhere. This combination hinders players from lifting their eyes to see how far the ball goes after contact.

 *See Section 4.26*

Balance, Balance, Balance

Assuming that you made contact with the ball, the key to being a consistent and productive hitter is maintaining balance. Balance should be stressed before, during, and after the swing. From the "nose over the toes" to the head staying down on contact, many ingredients in the hitting process work together to develop a well-balanced hitter.

One of the more fundamental aspects of hitting is bunting. When it comes to manufacturing runs and winning games, there may be no substitute for a player who can accurately execute a bunt.

Bunting

Squared vs. Pivot

 *See Section 4.27*

As I was progressing through my baseball career, from youth leagues until college, one approach to bunting was normally used. Before the ball was pitched, "squaring-up" to the pitcher was recommended. "Squaring-up" refers to the hitter coming out of the stance and facing the pitcher. Both feet are pointed at the pitcher, and the bat is extended out in front of the body to lay down a bunt. There were exceptions. The drag bunt requires an element of surprise, and for drag bunts squaring-up was not an option. A drag bunt is when the hitter sticks the bat out over the plate at the last second in hopes of catching the defense by surprise. A drag bunt followed by a sprint to first base was taught as the best way to bunt for a base hit. If you weren't bunting for a hit, and you needed to sacrifice the runner into scoring position, squaring-up to the plate was the recommended approach. There is a better way of bunting.

Figure 4.9 *Pivot position.*

An alternative to squaring-up when attempting a bunt is the "pivot" position. What is the pivot position? From the stance, the only movement required by the hitter is the squishing of the bug. Everything else stays the same as the traditional "squaring-up." When the pitcher delivers the ball, the hitter squishes the bug and places the bat in the hitting zone. Why the pivot as opposed to the squared-up position?

Young players are already scared of the baseball. Turning and facing the pitcher is intimidating! Watch a young player bunt and flinch or jump back as the ball is about to hit the bat. There's a psychological advantage to not facing the pitcher and just squishing the bug. It is far less threatening.

Another advantage is the decrease in movement before the ball is thrown. Allowing a player to move around in the batter's box before the pitch is risky and can be dangerous. The pivot only requires the movement of the back foot spinning. This movement also allows the hitter more time before having to reveal to the opposition that he or she is bunting.

If you are on a team that is aggressive and innovative, the "pivot" is great for fooling the opposition. Instead of bunting, it is easy to pull the bat back and slap at the ball for a hit-and-run or base hit.

 *See Section 4.28*

Hand Location

In bunting, hand location on the bat is important for control and safety. With the bat in the normal hitting grip, slide the top hand to the middle of the bat. A good location on the bat to place the top hand while bunting is the spot where you can balance the bat with just one hand. Make sure the fingers are behind the bat and not exposed to the ball. If the hand is completely around the bat, it could be hit (and hurt) by a pitched ball. For safety, be sure the fingers stay behind the bat. The bottom hand should grip the bat in the normal hitting position, or slightly above the knob. The objective is to be able to control the bat, while keeping the fingers protected.

Bat Angles

 See Section 4.29

Being able to place the ball down the third or first base line with the bunt is essential. The right hand is on the barrel of the bat, and the left hand is at the top of the grip. With the arms extended out in front of the plate, your bat now becomes a lever. To bunt the ball down the third base line, you simply need to pull your left hand back toward the body. The tip of the barrel is directed at the pitcher. For a bunt to first, the opposite holds true. Extend the left hand toward the pitcher, and move the barrel back toward the hitter.

Make sure your bat's barrel is above the hands when bunting the baseball. Players want to keep the bat level. Why have the barrel up? If the baseball is misaligned with the barrel level, the ball has a very good chance of popping into the air. Bunts should not go into the air! With the barrel above the hands (45 degrees), a slight miss will still result in a ground ball or foul straight back. When the barrel of the bat is raised, the chances of a player popping the ball up decrease.

Soft Hands

 See Section 4.30

When the ball is bunted, it should slow down and become difficult for the fielders to pick up and throw the hitter out at first. Making the ball slow down and "deadening" it require the bunter to use soft hands. As contact is being made, the hitter should pull back a little bit on the bat almost as though he's trying to catch the ball with the bat. This slight withdrawal or "give" of the bat will help deaden the ball down the line. Stabbing at the ball or pushing the bat outward only affords the fielders a better chance to pick up the bunt and throw a runner out. Be sure to "give a little" when bunting the baseball.

 *See Section 4.31*

> **Teaching Tip**
>
> Placing different colored hula-hoops down the baselines will not only help players bunt with accuracy, but now it becomes a game. Have the players try to bunt the ball and deaden it inside the hula-hoops. Allocate points for getting the ball in each colored hula-hoop, with the highest total winning the game. This is great for focusing and making bunting fun.

Grip It and Rip It

With all the mechanical requirements for hitting a baseball, it becomes overwhelming while at home plate to think of everything. When the hitter is in a game, one thing should be going through the mind: see it and hit it. All of the skills discussed in this chapter can be honed in practice or the off-season. By game time, they should be second nature. Practicing the skills over and over will integrate them into motor muscle memory.

Practice, Practice, Practice

It takes 1,000 perfect swings to change a bad habit. Perfect swings! Going out in the back yard and taking 100 swings isn't good enough. They should be 100 quality swings. Here is a challenge: take 100 swings a day for one year, or 365 days. At year's end, you will have swung the bat 36,500 times. How many players do you know who do this? These swings do not need to be on the field, off of a tee, or even with a bat. They can be dry swings in the bedroom with a small broomstick. No excuses. How long does it take to dry swing 100 times? It takes about 7 minutes. Hold yourself accountable and work on the skills everyday. I heard that Lance Berkman, star outfielder for the Houston Astros, used to take 150 swings as a right-hander, then 150 swings as a left-hander every day after school. His dad used to make him do it as a routine. His hard work has obviously paid off.

Situational Hitting

As much as bunting is important in manufacturing runs for a team, situational hitting might be more so. Knowing what to do with the bat at the plate and where to hit the ball should be in every hitter's mindset. Coaches will tell you that this ability and knowledge are a luxury. Most coaches would give talent away for hitters who can understand the game and execute the "situational hit."

Learning to situational hit involves studying the game and can be honed simply by watching hitters on TV. If there is a player on third with less than one out, a fly ball needs to be hit to the outfield. If there is a player on second with no outs, you want to hit the ball on the ground to the right side, so the runner can move to third. This knowledge is crucial to helping your team win games. It is also critical that you learn how to execute each of these swings in order to successfully accomplish the task.

Situational batting practice should be held during every practice session (refer to Chapter 13 for ways to do this). Most batting practices are run the same way. A player gets up to the plate, and the coach gives the player a designated number of swings while everyone shags the balls in the field. Inevitably, hitters will try to hit the ball as far as they can (go for homeruns), or swing at anything. Batting practice should be structured and held with a purpose. Every swing should be accounted for and executed to the best of the hitter's ability. No matter the age, situational hitting can be taught and learned—even by younger kids. It teaches game situations and shows players how to control the bat.

To be successful at the plate, a hitter must be willing to work hard on the fundamentals, and be aggressive in his approach. The hitter is entitled to three good swings at the plate . . . three. Don't get cheated at the plate by taking the first pitch. Make every swing count and "go hard or go home." The hitter should be thinking "strike" on every single pitch and develop an aggressive attitude. Be positive at the plate. Negative thinking will cause a hitter to become tentative and unsuccessful. Take responsibility for the results at the plate and never let excuses, for example, the pitcher, the judgment of the umpire, etc. become an easy way out.

The Winning Edge

Here are some other helpful tips to become a successful hitter:

- Have a game plan at the plate. Don't go up there hacking.
- Don't let negative people discourage you.
- You can fail 7 out of 10 times and be considered a winner.
- Battle at the plate . . . never give in to the pitcher.
- Always think about driving the ball up the middle when nobody is on base.
- Look for your pitch, that is, a ball in your "mashing zone."

Becoming a good hitter takes time, hard work, and good eye-hand coordination. Being able to hit will take a player far in baseball, even if you can't play defense. If a boy or girl can hit, teams will find a place in their starting line-up for that player.

Here is a story that sums up this chapter. There was a kid who was a very good youth league player. He loved to play defense, and had a really strong arm as a pitcher. He could hit very well, but as he got older had trouble adjusting to the speed of the game, and his hitting flaws started to catch up with him.

Hitting became more and more frustrating, and his dream was to play Division 1 baseball. People would laugh in disbelief at this desire, considering his remote northern location and small town. To make the dream even more unrealistic, nobody in his immediate family ever went to college.

In high school, he focused on defense and started at shortstop as a freshman on the varsity team. The coach, however, would have a designated hitter for him during the games because he just could not hit well.

The kid decided to devote his time to becoming a better hitter. He knew he needed to do this if he was ever going to play college baseball. He worked tirelessly in the off-season, quit all other sports, and would hit off a tee into a bed sheet. Often the player would hit outdoors in the snow, since there were no opportunities to join a gym or get baseball lessons.

Three years later, that player earned a Division 1 baseball scholarship at a southern university. He hit six home runs, drove in over thirty runs, and batted around .400 his senior year in high school earning numerous honors and awards. He went on to earn a varsity letter every year in college, and finished his collegiate career with a batting average over .300.

Who was this player? By now, you may have guessed it's me. I was never blessed with the natural ability to hit a baseball or supernatural eye-hand coordination. But I am living proof that working on the basics can lead to improvement. My hope is that anyone reading this book who has a dream to become a good hitter and play baseball at a higher-level will work to attain that goal. If you have trouble hitting, focus on developing the individual skills outlined above and in the next chapter.

CHAPTER 5

20 Hitting Flaws and How To Fix Them

TEACHING the hardest skill in sports (hitting) is not easy to do to a young mind. This chapter provides practical reinforcement for the basics of hitting by reviewing common hitting mistakes. Even when a flaw is obvious and the solution appears simple, correcting a hitter's mechanics and finding ways to store it in muscle memory are extremely difficult. The following drills are broken down into the four phases of hitting, which were described in Chapter 4. Each phase consists of common hitting errors and techniques to fix them.

1. Standing Incorrectly in the Batter's Box

Standing in the batter's box may sound unimportant. Yet, if hitters set up incorrectly, they are at a disadvantage before the ball is thrown. Moving too close to the plate can jam a hitter, while moving too far away eliminates plate coverage with the bat. When a player steps into the batter's box, make sure the player's bat can reach over the entire plate.

The second thing a hitter should do is find a good spot in the batter's box and stay there. Do not move up or back in the box. Learn the strike zone in the spot you choose and wait for the pitcher to throw a strike in that location. Do not chase pitches that are out of the strike zone. A good rule of thumb is to align the front foot with the front of the plate. If you draw a straight line along the top part of the plate, the front foot should be parallel with and be-

Phase I: The Stance

See Section 5.1

 *This symbol indicates reference to Companion DVD for video instruction*

hind the line. Setting up correctly at the plate is a good start to becoming a great hitter.

2. Choosing the Wrong Sized Bat

If the team uses a "community bat," where every player on the team shares the same bat, chances are it is not the right size for each player. Does it look too big in her hands when she swings it? Then it is too big. Does it look too small? Then it is too small. As long as a player is able to swing the bat with speed and control, the bat is right for that hitter.

Teaching Tip

Although using a heavier and longer bat produces more power, a lighter bat might be a wiser choice. Gary Sheffield uses a tree trunk for a bat, while Tony Gwynn used to swing a twig. While both arguably are great hitters, each had a different approach to hitting. Gary is incredibly strong and can swing a heavy, long bat, while Tony was more of a line drive hitter who excelled with incredible bat control. Choose a bat that matches your hitting style. If you are a power hitter, choosing a really light bat may not be the smartest choice. The key is to find a bat that is comfortable to swing, and allows for the most success at the plate.

---

3. Fear of the Ball

About a year ago a question was posed to me at a clinic. What do you do if a hitter is scared of the ball and is backing away from the plate? I told the person I had no idea and that I would get back to him after doing some research. Well, I researched, and researched, and researched some more. What was the result? Worry about the hitter who is not scared of the baseball! It is healthy for a young player to be scared of another human being throwing a hard object at him. It is normal. The player who stands in there fearlessly is unusual. What about the child who is scared? You must work on the fundamentals and convey to the batter that he or she is prepared and in control. With experience the fear will subside, and the hitter will be able to bat without inching backwards.

Figure 5.1 *A balanced stance.*

4. An Unbalanced Stance

 See Section 5.2

One key to hitting a baseball with power and consistency is balance. Without balance, a hitter loses a strong foundation and is susceptible to a pitcher's change of speeds. To fix this problem, have the hitter move the feet to at least shoulder-width apart. Telling players to get into a 3-point football stance is beneficial in teaching hitters to widen their stance. From this stance, push and pull the player to make sure he or she is balanced and able to withstand the exertion. After the feet are balanced, a short stride should be taken when meeting the ball.

A good drill for fixing an unbalanced stance is with a basketball. While the hitter is in the stance, take a basketball and put it between the legs. With a squeezing motion ask the player to keep the ball positioned above the knees, and then take a few swings off a tee.

5. Improper Grip

 See Section 5.3

The lifeline between the bat and the hitter is the hands. Without a proper grip on the bat, the chances of being successful drop. If a hitter is told to swing hard, chances are the player will squeeze the bat tighter and "choke" the bat. Remember, the hands are a "lifeline." That is, they should enliven the bat, not kill it with a "death grip." Choking restricts the flow of the hands and diminishes their whipping action.

The first thing a hitter needs to do is line up the knocking knuckles. Remember, there are two sets of knuckles: "knocking knuckles" (the ones you use to knock on a door), and "punching knuckles" (the ones you use for throwing a punch). When the punching knuckles are aligned, the movement of the bat and wrists is restricted, producing a slow bat. The knocking knuckles, when lined up, allow the wrists to be free and generate a whipping action with the bat. It's important to learn the knocking knuckle grip. A good way to teach lining up the knocking knuckles is to place the bat on the ground barrel down between your feet. Reach down with both hands and grip the bat. Bring the bat up to your shoulder, and the knocking knuckles should be aligned.

Another problem associated with the grip is having the bat too deep in the hands. The deeper in the hands, the deeper trouble you are in. The bat should be held in the fingers, not the hands. This grip should give the sensation that the bat is going to fly out of the hands at any moment. The knocking knuckles grip permits the bat to whip through the zone.

 *See Section 5.4*

6. Poor Vision (self-inflicted)

Hitting a baseball is hard enough. Doing it with impaired vision is nearly impossible! Yet some hitters partially blind themselves at the plate. The player will look familiar. He is the one who stands at the plate with his head tucked deep in his front shoulder, or tilts his head to the side and looks at the pitcher sideways. In order to be a successful hitter at the plate, a player must look at the pitcher with both eyes. Fixing this problem is easy if the player understands his or her problem. If they don't understand, put your hand over the front eye in the stance, or the one closer to the pitcher. An eye patch can even be worn to emphasize the point. In the stance, the hitter should be able to see the pitcher with the back eye, that is, the right eye for a right-handed batter.

Teaching Tip

Placing an eye-patch, or some other obstruction, over the eye closer to the pitcher is a good way to check a hitter's vision. If the eye closer to the catcher cannot see the pitcher, a player needs to turn the head so the pitcher can be seen clearly.

---

1. Stride is Too Long

A long stride shortens the amount of time it takes for a hitter to make a decision whether or not to swing. The more time a hitter has to make a decision, the higher the probability of success. The stride should be small, with the feet shoulder-width apart.

Figure 5.2 *Adjusting the stride.*

Another component to the stride is getting the foot flat but staying on the balls of the feet. Striding onto the tip of the toe creates an unstable base. Get the foot down soon, stay flat, and keep the weight of the body on the balls of the feet.

Fixing the over-stride can be done with a broomstick or bat. Place the stick 3–4 inches in front of the hitter's stride foot and ask the player to take some swings. If the stride is too long, the player will step on the stick. A smaller stride will not cause the hitter to lose power. If anything, the hitter will notice more power and consistency from the swing, when done correctly.

2. Hands are Not Loading Up . . . Weight is Going Forward

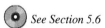

To have a quick and powerful bat, the hitter needs to load up and take the hands back. How far the hitter takes the hands back depends on ability and comfort. The distance can be as little as one inch to a foot depending on arm length and preference. As the stride foot goes forward, the hands should simultaneously load back. Remember to keep the head stationary. At the same time, the torso should not go forward or backward.

The image of a boxer hitting an opponent is great for explaining the load-up phase of hitting. To be quick and powerful, a boxer must take the hands back before throwing a punch. If the hands do not go back, the punch will not produce power. Hitters who do not go back with the hands, or recoil, usually have trouble with faster pitching and are singles hitters at best.

A good drill for loading up and keeping the torso and head still is the fishing drill. Hang a bobber from the ceiling using fishing line. Get in the stance and align the bobber with the hitter's nose. Take some dry swings focusing on loading up and taking the hands back. If the nose is too far in front of or behind the bobber, the head is moving too much. The weight is getting too far out on the front foot or the upper body is leaning back too much. This is a great drill to do during inclement weather.

 *See Section 5.7*

3. Bat Wrap

While taking the hands back in the load-up phase, players have a tendency to raise the hands and extend the bat behind the head. This "bat wrap" leads to several problems in the swing.

The first thing bat wrap does is create a longer distance until impact with the ball. Ideally, the path from bat head to ball should be as short as possible. The track from behind the head onto the swing plane may be the longest possible. Bat wrap increases the time it takes to swing and thus makes the batter vulnerable to a hard thrower. Unless you have lightning-fast hands and ninja reflexes, wrapping the bat will increase the probability of getting jammed or not getting around in time to hit the ball.

Another thing bat wrap causes is front arm barring. When a player wraps the bat around the head, the arms want to extend quicker than normal, which produces a hitter I call "the spinner." This is a person who rotates the upper torso and swings with the shoulders. In this swing the upper body "spins" to make the bat go through the zone. Both arms are extended too early, and the front shoulder and head pull away from the plate. It is tough to hit a ball with the head pulled, the shoulders opened early, and the arms extended. Usually the bat is not in the hitting zone very long.

How do you fix bat wrap? With a wall behind you while in the stance, load up and pretend a pitcher is throwing to you. The wall should be close enough (maybe 2–3 feet) so that you can touch the top of the bat against the wall. The bat striking the wall will reinforce taking the bat straight back and not wrapping it around the head. Be sure not to "flatten the bat" completely. Flattening the bat means straightening it out so that it is parallel to the ground. The barrel should tip back only slightly when loading up. Too much flattening of the bat decreases the bat action necessary to produce torque and whip.

4. Hitting Off of the Front Foot

 *See Section 5.8*

When loading up, it is important the stride leg straightens when the hitter is about to start the swing. Why? I have posed this question to coaches and players at clinics and have never received a good answer.

Once the stride foot lands, it should not move. Many hitters land on their toes. Some hitters are gifted enough to do this and it feels comfortable. It is a preferred movement, but it is not recommended. When the stride foot hits the ground, it should be flat . . . on the ball of the foot, but flat. Keeping the nose over the toes helps keep the weight on the balls of the feet, and this will produce a balanced stance. Show players how easy it is to push someone standing on their toes, in comparison to pushing a person balanced on the balls of the feet. A flat foot produces a balanced stance.

The stride leg should straighten out when the foot hits the ground. This leg straightens to keep your weight from going forward. At the same time, it forms a solid base from which to swing. With the weight from the back foot transferring to the front with a lot of force, the lead leg stiffens to produce a prop. A good analogy would be putting something against a door to keep it from opening. The front leg allows the back leg and hips to explode and prevents the torso and head from moving forward. This action produces a balanced swing and keeps the weight from going forward too fast.

In order to correct hitting off the front foot, hang a bobber or some other small, light object from the ceiling. The bobber should be aligned with the nose in the stance and hung about a foot away from the hitter. The hitter should load up and swing the bat and check to make sure the head is not too far in front of or behind the bobber. The idea is to try to keep the head motionless and yet generate explosiveness with the lower body. Stiffening the front leg helps accomplish this objective. To make this drill even more effective, place a basketball between the legs to reinforce good balance.

 *See Section 5.9*

5. Stepping Out or "In the Bucket"

"Stepping in the bucket" occurs when a hitter takes an initial stride toward third base. The correct approach with the stride foot should be directly toward the pitcher. Hitters will sometimes open the front foot and "step out" when swinging the bat.

Stepping in the bucket creates a number of other problems. The hitter can't cover the plate with the bat because he or she pulls the body away from home plate. Power is lessened because the hips open too fast.

There's a fairly simple way to correct stepping in the bucket. Get a broomstick or some other long object, and place it approximately 6–8 inches behind the lead foot while in the stance. When the hitter strides while loading up, the lead foot should not step on the stick or across it. This drill can be done using tees, soft toss, or on the field during batting practice. For some reason, players will not step in the bucket if an object is there to remind them not to. Over time, with the help of muscle memory, the skill will be done automatically and the problem solved.

Teaching Tip

It takes doing something 1,000 times perfectly before it is stored into motor muscle memory. Motor muscle memory is when the muscles perform without thinking, as they do when walking or moving a bike (once the skills have been learned over time). If the activity is not done perfectly, the process is reinforced incorrectly and produces a flaw that's hard to change. In this context, to swing perfectly means to swing without the flaws.

 *See Section 5.10*

6. Lead Foot Opens Toward Pitcher Too Soon

When taking a stride, the front foot should land and stay closed. "Staying closed" means that the toes are not pointing toward the pitcher, but rather are pointing toward home plate. Many players open their lead foot and when it lands, point the toes at the pitcher. In doing so, the hitter opens up the front hips early, thereby losing power. This hitting flaw also triggers the front shoulder to open prematurely. In general, opening the lead foot causes the front side to fly open. After the hitter has finished with bat extension, the front foot will open up and the hitter can run to first base. At no time should this be taught. This action will occur naturally after hitting the baseball.

One way to fix the problem of opening the lead foot is to tell the hitter to "take the heel to the pitcher." This does not mean that the heel must actually point toward the pitcher with the toes facing back toward the catcher. The toes should still face home plate, but the heel leads toward the pitcher. The foot will land closed when this type of stride is taken.

1. Casting or Barring the Front Arm

In the past, players were taught to get the arms extended in order to hit well. While extension is important, some of the details were left out on *when* extension is supposed to take place. Extending the arms too soon is called "casting." The motion looks like a fisherman casting a rod. It is also commonly called "barring" the front arm, because the lead arm straightens out like a bar or rod.

Let's conduct an experiment. Put two boxers in the ring to spar against one another. Lets call them Boxer A and Boxer B. We are going to take Boxer A's arms, put splints on them, and tape them so they're straight. Boxer B will have the arms free, no splints attached. Who do you think is going to win? Boxer A with the great premature arm extension, or Boxer B who can move his elbows to create lever action?

Arm extension is important at the point of contact or *directly after* contact. In other words, to hit the ball with speed and power, the arms should not be extended until contact is made or right after contact. Straightening out the arms too early lessens the strength and power of the swing. It usually involves rotating the shoulders and produces a lot of ground balls and hitters getting jammed.

Another tip for eliminating casting is to keep the hands inside the baseball. As the ball is sitting on a tee or arriving from the pitcher after thrown, a hitter should swing at the ball with the hands never going outside the ball. If an imaginary line was drawn from the pitcher to the catcher through the center of the baseball, then the hands should never cross that imaginary line. With the hands inside the baseball, the arms will not get extended too early.

There are exceptions. A hitter who falls backward after (or even during) the swing might be getting the arms extended early but

Phase III: The Swing

 *See Section 5.11*

leans backward to make sure the barrel is in the hitting zone. The hands remain inside that imaginary line only because the hitter leans to keep the hands inside the ball. In effect, the player over-compensates for the bad mechanics, but loses balance and power.

Do you have a player on your team who pulls the ball about 50 feet foul (or more)? The first thought is that the swing is too fast! So the coach may think the pitcher's not throwing hard enough. So the next pitch is a little harder, and the hitter gets jammed. The coach throws another pitch a little slower, and the hitter pulls the ball 50 feet foul . . . and the cycle continues. The hitter is "front arm barring," "hitting around the baseball," or getting his arms extended too early. This is also called "casting." As the ball comes through the zone, the hitter makes contact in front of the plate and pulls it foul. If the hitter does not get the bat through the zone in time, the hitter gets jammed. Put a hitter in the stance with the arms extended straight out over the plate. Take a look at what part of the bat is covering home plate. The "sweet spot," or fat part of the bat, isn't even in the strike zone! To move that "sweet spot" into the zone, the hitter must push the bat farther ahead of the plate to make contact. This usually produces a foul ball due to the bat angle from the hitter. The problem is not the hitter's swing speed. Rather, the swing is too long.

The most effective drill to correct casting is the double-tee drill. For this drill, you need two tees. Place the first tee in a position to hit the ball down the middle (which is right in front of home plate in the center). Place the other tee on the outside point on home plate opposite of the hitter. It is the point where the sides of the plate come together to form an angle.

Place a baseball on the tee set up down the middle, and a tennis ball on the back tee. The object is, first, to hit the baseball down the middle. If on the same swing the tennis ball is hit, the front arm is barring and "casting" is taking place. The hands should stay inside the baseball and drive it up the middle with a normal swing. This is an excellent drill to use for an inside pitch, down the middle pitch, and outside pitch. The front tee will need to be repositioned to work on each of these pitches.

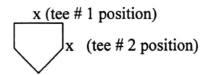

Another effective drill if a ball or hitting area is not available to the hitter is the "face-the-fence" drill. Find a wall or fence and face it with a bat in your hands. Extend the bat with the end of the barrel resting against the wall and the knob of the bat against your chest. This is the distance away from the wall a hitter should be in order to do the drill. While facing the wall, get in the stance. The imaginary pitcher will not be throwing from the wall the hitter is facing. The wall serves as an obstruction if a long swing is taken. Take a normal swing, and if the bat hits the ball, the swing is not a short, compact swing and the hitter is hitting around the baseball, or casting. I recommend doing this in front of an obstruction that either will not be damaged when hit or can be damaged, such as a piece of cardboard. The same thing goes for the bat. If the wall is hit, the bat could be damaged. Doing this drill in front of a cardboard box or some other soft obstruction is recommended.

Teaching Tip

Players should learn to throw the knob of the bat toward the ball. If the pitch is inside, the player will throw the hands and knob directly to the ball on the inner part of the plate. If the pitch is outside, the player will throw the knob toward the outer half of the plate, while still keeping the hands inside the ball. Throwing the knob toward the ball will keep the swing short and compact, and still keep the hands inside the ball. It is important to get the barrel through the zone and make contact at the appropriate location for each pitch.

---

2. Looping/Dipping/Upper-cutting

 *See Section 5.12*

A very common flaw among youth hitters, upper-cutting, is not a new flaw to the seasoned coach. Upper-cutting, looping, and dipping all refer to the hitter dropping the hands and back elbow, which in turn creates an upward swing trajectory. This flaw usually produces a lot of fly balls for outs.

Let's draw a triangle while in the stance from the knob of the bat (point A), to 8 inches below the back elbow (point B), to where contact is made with the ball (point C). Taking a route from Point A to Point B to Point C with the swing is looping, dipping, or upper cutting. The route produces a long swing and a bad approach to hitting the baseball. The shortest distance between two points is a straight line. By understanding and applying that geometrical principle, you can show your players that taking the bat from Point A to Point C generates the quickest swing when hitting the ball.

The most effective way to get rid of an upper cut is to use another version of the double-tee drill. For this drill, place one tee in front of home plate for a pitch down the middle. The second tee is stationed where home plate comes to a point on the back. With a baseball sitting on the tee in front, place another baseball (a tennis ball is safer) on the back tee. In the normal hitting position, take swings trying to hit the baseball off the front tee. If the back ball (tennis ball) is hit, there is a loop in the hitter's swing. Repeated swings done correctly will help the hitter develop a "Point A to Point C"swing.

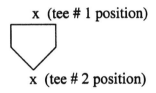

x (tee # 1 position)

x (tee # 2 position)

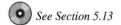 *See Section 5.13*

3. Rolling Wrists Over Before or During Contact

In the past, coaches would stress how important it was to snap the wrists upon impact. The wrists, according to some, were considered the key to hitting with power. This is false. Rolling the wrists over, either before or during contact, is wrong. This action causes the hitter to lose a lot of power when making contact with the baseball. Strong wrists are important, but only when used correctly.

For optimal power, the hands must be palm up/palm down upon impact. This positioning of the hands allows the hitter to use more force when moving the bat through the hitting zone.

To prove the point and feel the power, instruct a hitter to grab a bat and get in the stance. Stand in front of the player, and have him or her imitate a swing and freeze at the impact point. The first time should be done with the wrists rolling over. With force, you should then push the bat back as the hitter tries to resist. The second time, tell the batter to swing with the palm up/palm down technique and then freeze the swing. Again, apply the force to the bat and ask the hitter to resist. Hitters will definitely see and feel the difference between the two theories and understand the importance of the palm up/palm down wrist position.

See Section 5.14

Teaching Tip

Possessing strong wrists is essential to hitting the ball with power. A good way to build up strength is to use a wrist roller. There are conventional tools on the market that accomplish this task, but one can be made using a dowel rod, rope, and a light weight. Purchase a small, thick dowel rod (about 18 inches long). Drill a hole in the center, and thread the rope through the hole. Tie a knot so the end of the rope doesn't slip through the hole. At the other end of the rope, tie a 5 pound weight. The player grasps the dowel rod and can roll the weight up, and also let the weight down in a slow, controlled manner. Make sure the arms are extended and the wrists are doing the work. The amount of repetitions depends on the strength and conditioning of the player. The exercise can be done with the hands palm up, or palm down.

---

4. Not Squishing the Bug

See Section 5.15

To use the legs and hips to hit with power, a player must squish the bug. "Squish the bug" refers to the back foot spinning or pivoting to clear the hips and drive with the legs. As the hands come forward to start the swing, the back foot starts to pivot or spin allowing the back leg and hips to generate power. In the absence of this movement, the hips cannot open up and thereby allow the hands to come through fast. In the right position, the inner part of the back leg is used for power. The legs are much stronger from the front than from the side. If this weren't the case, NFL linemen would line up across from one another side by side rather than head-on.

It is very important not to over-squish the bug. This happens when a hitter over-rotates on the back foot and balance is lost. The foot should end up in a position that resembles a sprinter about to take off from the starting blocks. The back leg should be in an "L" position, with the torso "staying tall" and not bent over at the waist.

An effective drill for teaching players to squish the bug is by starting from the squished bug position. With the player already loaded up and squishing the bug, the hitter should take normal swings. This drill can be done taking batting practice, soft toss, or off of a tee. When that feels comfortable, have the hitter bat from the normal position and emphasize squishing the bug.

Figure 5.4 *Squishing the bug.*

See Section 5.16

5. Pulling the Head/Front Shoulder

One of the most common hitting flaws at any level, but especially at the youth level, is pulling the head or front shoulder. When the hitter goes to take a swing, the head and lead shoulder start the swing as opposed to the hands and elbows. As the hands and elbows continue through the hitting zone, the head and lead shoulder seem to be attached together on a string. They continue to move with the hands, eventually pulling away from the ball. This flaw also occurs because hitters are habitually looking up after contact to see where the ball is going to land.

If you can't see it, how can you hit it? Pulling the head has obvious consequences. A player who pulls the head usually opens the front shoulder too early. We call these players "spinners." Instead of throwing the hands to the ball with the swing short and compact, the hitter uses the upper body to try to accelerate the swing. It is hard to generate a lot of bat speed using the spinning motion of the upper body.

The best drill for teaching hitters to keep the shoulder closed and head down on the ball is hitting from the tee. When a player hits the baseball, the head should stay on the spot where contact is made, that is, on the tee. The hitter should not look up to see where the ball has gone, so this drill is optimal to do in front of a net or screen. Eventually motor muscle memory will take over, and the head will remain down with the shoulder for all hitting activities. Remember, it takes 1,000 perfect swings to change a bad habit (be sure to wear batting gloves . . . all those swings produce blisters!).

Teaching Tip

The phrase "Mike to Ike" is often used to reinforce keeping the head down on the ball. The lead shoulder is called "Mike," and the shoulder closer to the catcher is called "Ike." The player starts the chin at Mike as the ball is thrown, and finishes with the chin at Ike after the swing is completed. Make sure the chin doesn't touch either shoulder when following this tip. The chin should start in the proximity of Mike and end in the general area of Ike. Tucking the chin against the shoulders creates stiffness in the upper body.

---

1. Incorrect Bat Extension

Phase IV: The Follow-through

 *See Section 5.17*

Watching a professional baseball game on TV is enjoyable. It is amazing to see world class athletes with phenomenal mechanics excelling at a game that is difficult to play. However, I can see how coaches and players are misled when watching these hitters at the plate. With unbelievable bat speed, hitters swing at fastballs moving in excess of 90 mph. On television, the swing looks fairly slow, and the players make it appear effortless. The average fan sees the hitter start the swing, then follow through with the bat ending up behind the hitter's head or torso.

To the average eye, following through seems to occur some-where in back of the hitter. Therefore, imitating professionals, young hitters swing by pulling the hands away from the zone and trying to get extension somewhere behind the head or torso. The problem is that a step was missed. The young player takes a short-cut to the final destination.

Two boxers stand across from one another. As Boxer A hits Boxer B, he makes contact with him and continues as if moving his hand *through* Boxer B. This "continuing through" provides a lot of power in the punch. If Boxer B returns a punch, but upon impact quickly pulls his glove behind himself, do you think the punch will have the same effect as Boxer A's punch?

Upon impact with the baseball, the extension and path of the bat should be out in front or through the baseball. Hitters must not hurry to complete the swing in a trophy pose. If they do so, the hands will take a path that cheats and finish too early. The hands, upon contact, should continue through the ball and extend out in front of the plate. Only after full extension is achieved should the bat continue around and behind the body. The swing happens so fast on TV, which makes it difficult, if not impossible, to see the swing path extend out and *through* the ball, and then, as a final movement, around the body.

There are two good drills to help reinforce this action. The first drill I call the "The Kung Fu." In martial arts movies, actors often perform slow, mechanical moves. The moves are done very slowly, so that when it comes time to move fast, the muscles have practiced the motions and understand the correct path. The Kung Fu drill in baseball serves the same purpose. Without a bat and in the stance, the hands assume a position as though actually holding a bat. The hitter slowly loads up, and takes an imaginary swing with the hands. Here is the interesting part for coaches. Stand behind the hitter and watch where the hands go. They should extend forward and finish out in front and circle around. Players who don't follow through correctly will get to the contact point and pull the hands back behind the body. This drill can be done anywhere.

A second effective corrective is a soft-toss drill from behind the hitter. With the hitter standing at the plate in the stance, the feeder (person flipping the ball to the hitter) is positioned behind the hitter or directly behind home plate. The feeder tosses the ball from behind the plate and through the strike zone. The ball should be tossed hard enough that it doesn't drop from loss of velocity until after it passes the hitter. The hitter will wait for the ball and try to hit it just after it passes into the zone. This drill is great for teaching the hitter to get extension. If the hands wrap around the body with poor extension, it is impossible to hit the baseball. This drill also makes the hitter throw the hands faster. The swing can't be started early or the ball will be missed. The hitter will have to be patient and really fire the hands as the ball travels into the hitting zone.

> ## Teaching Tip
>
> Hitting off a tee in slow motion is an effective way to teach the muscles to get correct extension. Instead of swinging hard at the ball, slow down the swing and slowly knock the ball off the tee and finish the swing in slow motion. This is a good way to improve the entire swing, not just extension. The player can focus on the proper fundamentals and correct a flaw that may be reoccurring.

2. Not Finishing the Swing

See Section 5.18

A hitter who makes contact with the baseball, but immediately stops the bat upon impact is difficult to miss on the baseball diamond. This hitter usually makes contact, but the ball doesn't leave the infield.

After impact with the baseball, the bat must go through the ball for optimal power. If this is explained to the hitter, the player may recognize and change the habit. If not, the analogy of a boxer throwing a punch and extending through a person can be effective. It can even be demonstrated in slow motion (don't actually throw a hard punch, but visually show and explain the theory).

If these remedies do not work, the last resort (and the most fun) is to take "the plunge." Take a plunger (a clean one) and put the stick end of the plunger into a tee that has a hole in it. These are usually the tees that have the rubber post in the middle of the plate (which is the incorrect spot by the way for a pitch down the middle). The wooden stick will slide into the post, and the rubber cup end of the plunger will be exposed. This rubber end serves as a giant tee. Place a partially flattened basketball (or any other large ball) on the plunger end. Get in the stance and swing away. Players love to wallop the basketball, and a hitter who stops on impact won't hit the basketball very far. The plunger drill is not only good for correcting this flaw, but it will be one of the players' favorite drills.

3. Lose Balance After the Swing

See Section 5.19

Balance is the key to hitting a baseball with power and consistency. At any given time, a hitter could hit a baseball hopping on one leg or even swinging with one arm. But to hit consistently and with power, a hitter must maintain a balanced foundation throughout the hitting process.

An effective way to work on balance is by dry swinging. "Dry swinging" refers to taking swings without hitting a ball. A hitter goes through the four phases of hitting without touching a ball. While dry swinging, a hitter can focus on staying balanced throughout the entire swing. After swinging, the hitter should freeze and hold the follow-through with complete balance.

Another way to work on balance is to progress through the phases of hitting in segments. For this drill, call out the phases of the hitting process. When each phase is called, the hitter should demonstrate that segment. For example, the coach calls out "number 1." The hitter gets in a good, balanced stance. A call of "number 2" would initiate the load-up phase. With "3" the hitter would swing the bat. Since 3 and 4 are hard to do in segments (4 is the follow-through), the call of "4" is a hop in the air. Why a hop? If the swing phase is balanced, then a hop in the air should place the feet back down where the hitter finished the swing.

Teaching Tip

The four phases of the hitting drill described above can be done with the entire team at once. Gather all of the players in the outfield, and call out the numbers. The coaching staff can walk around and observe all of the players to make sure the correct mechanics are being used. This is a great team hitting drill and can be done regularly at practice.

Fixing Hitting Problems: An Overview

Hitting is a matter of techniques. These can be done properly or incorrectly. Usually, bad technique is a result of bad habits. In some respects, especially with younger players, it is just as important to nip bad habits in the bud, as it is to demonstrate proper technique.

This chapter has covered numerous flaws, which if eliminated, will put your players on the path to mastering hitting and deriving more fun from the game.

CHAPTER 6

Infielding

PITCHING and defense win championships. While hitting gets all the glamour, there is no substitute for good defense. The pitcher and the whole team are more effective when balls are caught and thrown properly. Indeed, the more readily outs are made, by pitchers or fielders, the fewer chances the other team has to score runs.

Fielding a ground ball and executing outs incorporate techniques, just as hitting does. With good footwork and proper technique, fielding can be improved, and a player can excel at his or her position.

Fielding a baseball requires a positive attitude. Confidence is essential. Doubt will have an adverse affect on fielding. With that in mind, having the attitude that every ball is going to be hit to you is important. Indeed, fielders should want this. Thinking the ball is always going to be hit your way and knowing the situation improve the chances of executing a play successfully.

Another way a player can get an edge on the competition is to read each pitch in relation to the batter's technique. The location of the pitches from the pitcher and the swing of the batter can tip the fielder on where the ball has a good probability of being hit. If a right-handed hitter has a tendency to hit the baseball to the left side of the field, and the pitcher is throwing the ball inside, chances are the ball is going to be hit to the shortstop or third baseman. Fielders who adjust their position to where the ball is likely to be hit have a definite advantage.

Mental Approach

This symbol indicates reference to Companion DVD for video instruction

Lastly, nobody wants to make errors, but they are inevitable. There is not a player alive, youth to professional, who has not made an error while playing defense. Turning the error into a learning experience and not a traumatic one is crucial to a player's psyche. Learning from the mistake and keeping a positive attitude will help your chances of making the next play.

Approach (Before the Ball is Fielded)

Communication

Nothing's sweeter to a fan's ears than a team that talks to one another. This does not refer to the traditional chatter that occurs on the field like "let's go" or "hey batter, hey batter." Communication is what prepares a team for each and every fielding scenario.

The catcher is traditionally the quarterback of the team and sets the tone. After every batter, the catcher should step in front of home plate and yell the number of outs and where the ball should be thrown in each situation. Not only should the catcher speak out, but the fielders should acknowledge, and if necessary repeat, the remarks. This reduces the likelihood of a player not knowing how many outs there are or where to go with the ball once it is hit. This interaction among players is effective. It helps players know what to do if the ball is hit to them.

 *See Section 6.1*

Setting Up

Before the pitcher throws, the fielder should move into a good athletic position. The hands should not be on the knees, nor should the player be bent over with the glove on the ground. In both of these positions, the fielder will inevitably waste time standing up when the ball is hit. Before the pitcher goes into the wind-up, the infielder should be playing a little deeper than normal on the field. As the pitcher goes into the wind-up, the fielder's momentum should be moving towards home plate. This could be small steps forward, for instance, a "left foot, right foot, left foot" structured movement. As the ball arrives at the hitter, a shuffle of the feet or a slight hop needs to be taken.

Watch a tennis match on television. Before the server hits the ball, the receiving player shifts back and forth. As the serve is hit, the receiver takes a small hop. To accelerate towards the ball, the infielder, like the tennis player, needs to get the feet moving, just as the batter is swinging. This enables the player to react more rapidly and also increases his or her range.

"Dancing with the Baseball"

 *See Section 6.2*

When a ground ball is hit, the fielder must be both aggressive and yet under control. As the baseball bounces across the infield, the player will have to make a decision on how to field it. Being able to read the hop and predict the ball's action are possible—if the eye is trained to do so. This is referred to as "dancing with the baseball." The player allows the ball to be a "dance partner," and lets it guide him or her in coming together. Bouncing ball and moving fielder are "in sync." If the ball travels through the infield without taking any hops, the fielder can time the ball and make an easy play. If the ball starts hopping along the ground and doesn't roll on the ground to the player, a different decision needs to be made. A fielder times the ball's arrival according to the type of hop he or she identifies. At that point, the player chooses the hop to go for. Just before the player fields the ball, he or she needs to break down and get the body under control. Often, players are too aggressive, overrun the baseball, and have no control over their body. There are three types of hops to choose from right before the fielder breaks down: the long hop, short hop, or "in-betweener."

The long hop is sometimes called "the gravy hop." It's the ball that takes a long easy bounce, the kind of ground ball an infielder wants. If it's an option, the fielder will accelerate forward and field the ball on the long hop.

The short hop is a little more difficult than the long hop, but is still not a bad choice. This ball takes a hop and hits the ground right before it goes into the glove. Infielders may pull their head up when the short hop is fielded. Tell players to stay disciplined and keep the head down on this hop. The glove should be kept close to the ground for the short hop.

The in-betweener is not favored and often feared. It happens when the batter hits the ball so hard the fielder has little time to react, much less make a choice. As the ball rockets across the infield, choosing the hop is not an option. An "in-betweener" is a ball that is not a short hop, nor is it a long hop. It is somewhere between the two. A fielder is not sure whether to sprint forward or retreat. The best way to field an in-betweener is to relax and not tighten the muscles. Staying relaxed allows the muscles to react fluidly. While the in-betweener cannot be chosen, it is a type of hop that must be practiced, since it inevitably occurs in games. "Dancing with the baseball" allows a player to develop a sense of rhythm and timing with the baseball. It also gives the fielder a sense of where the optimal place may be to move to field the ball. Developing rhythm, choosing the hop, and being aggressive and also under control are all important ingredients that allow a fielder to be successful.

Fielding the Ball
As the ball is about to arrive, fielders must instinctively use the proper fundamentals. When the fundamentals are not applied, the margin for error increases. The key to being a good fielder is consistency, and the following skills will enable a player to be reliable on the field.

See Section 6.3

Lowering the Tailgate

When fielding the baseball, a player must "lower the tailgate." Coaches refer to this as "getting the butt down." On a field or during a game, the phrase sounds vulgar and distasteful. "Lowering the tailgate" sounds better. The knees should be bent, the weight should be on the balls of the feet, and the knees should be inside the feet. This position resembles the three point stance in football. The feet should be at least shoulder-width apart, and the player needs to be well balanced.

Figure 6.1 *Lowering the tailgate.*

See Section 6.4

Staggering the Feet

With the tailgate lowered, the glove-side foot should be slightly farther forward than the throwing-side foot. For a right-handed player, the left foot is positioned a little ahead of the right foot. The ball should be fielded off the leading foot, or the glove-side.

Fielding the Ball

There are two reasons why the ball should be fielded in this location. The staggering of the feet allows the right foot to cross in
front of the left to throw to the desired location (this is in reference
to a right-handed player). Shuffling of the feet or taking too many
slide-steps wastes time and gives the runner more time to beat the
throw to the base. Once the ball is fielded, a "right-left" foot action
allows the fielder to get rid of the ball faster.

The second reason is less obvious. If a bad hop occurs, the
fielder is in a better position to knock the ball down. For a
right-handed player, a bad hop to the left allows the fielder to
knock the ball down with the glove. Since the player is fielding the
ball off the left foot, the glove is in close proximity to make a play
on the ball quicker. A bad hop to the right will hit the player in the
chest. This knocks the ball down, keeps the ball in front, and gives
the player a chance to make a play. If the ball is fielded improperly
off the right foot, and the ball kicks badly to the left, the body will
be in a position to knock the ball down. But if the ball takes a bad
bounce to the right, the glove has to travel across the body, and is
not close enough to knock the ball down.

Elbows Bent

 See Section 6.5

The elbows should be bent when a player is fielding the baseball. With the elbows bent, the arms can move quicker. Straighten
the arms out and lock the elbows and try to move quickly back and
forth. Now perform the same back and forth motion using bent
elbows. The bent elbows are much quicker and more athletic.

Hands

See Section 6.6

Good hands are important in fielding. "Good hands" means
hands that are relaxed and pull back a little when receiving the
ball. As the ball goes into the glove, the hands relax and "soften"
slightly to absorb the impact. Bounce a ball off a wall and watch
how hard it rebounds. The same effect occurs when a player stabs
at the ball and doesn't pull back a little upon impact.

The proper positioning of the hands can be related to the
numbers on a clock. The glove hand should be under the ball
positioned at seven o'clock, and the throwing hand should be next

to the glove and positioned at two o'clock. The reason for the throwing hand to be in this position is twofold. The first is so the hand can cover the fielded ball and make sure it stays in the glove. The second reason is rapid hand transfer. With the throwing hand resting on the ball, a quick throw is possible. In addition, the hand position allows more time to rotate the ball into a four-seam grip.

Figure 6.2 *Hand position.*

 *See Section 6.7*

Head Down

As the batted ball approaches the glove, the fielder should look the ball into the glove. Many players lift the head too soon to see where they intend to throw. As the ball is looked into the glove, the head should remain down. Tell players that the bead on the top of a fielder's the cap should be visible when that player is catching a groundball.

 *See Section 6.8*

Working Through the Ball

Many times when the ball is fielded players remain stationary. Their momentum is not moving through the baseball. As the ball is caught, the player must continue to move through the ball and toward the intended target. This movement allows fielders to decrease the distance between them and their intended target. Momentum also allows the player to make a stronger throw, since throwing a ball from a stationary position produces less velocity.

Throwing the Ball Throwing errors may be the most common reason for lost games in youth baseball. Players will make good plays when fielding the ball, but full execution requires the fielder to then make an accurate throw. Coaches and players alike assume that throwing a baseball is a skill that everyone can perform. In fact, as was stressed in Chapter 3, throwing a ball is a skill with numerous elements that must be learned.

Four-seam Grip

See Section 6.9

The four-seam grip allows the baseball to travel in a straight line due to aerodynamics (refer to chapter 3 for more detail on the four-seam grip). During a game there is not enough time to check the grip after the ball is caught. The player must field the ball and throw quickly. Gripping the ball with four seams needs to become an unconscious habit. How is this accomplished?

The blind can read. They cannot see the words, but the invention of Braille allowed people who cannot see the chance to read using the sense of touch. The fielder can learn an invaluable lesson from the blind. A baseball is constructed with raised seams. Flip the ball in the air repeatedly and practice rotating it until a four-seam grip is attained without thinking. Once this becomes a habit, the hand positioned at two o'clock, which covers the fielded ball, can instantly rotate it into a four-seam grip before the throw.

Lining Up the Scope

See Section 6.10

A fielder's footwork and body positioning are as important as the glove and throwing arm. The ball can be fielded and the player can have a strong arm, but if the body is not positioned correctly an errant throw will result. The fielder must line up the lead shoulder with the target when making a throw. The lead shoulder is the "scope," and the arm is the "gun." With the lead shoulder lined up with the target, the throw will have a better chance of hitting the target. (See chapter 3 for more information on "the scope.")

To line up the scope once the ball is fielded, the player must rotate the torso and use good footwork. Many players throw the ball with the chest leading to the target. This not only increases the chances of a poor throw, but also puts undue stress on the rotator cuff, which could lead to shoulder problems.

Short C versus Long C

See Section 6.11

Earlier the "long C" was discussed. It is important for young players to use this motion when throwing a baseball. The "long C" refers to a long throwing motion that takes a path resembling the letter "C". The path of the ball travels down by the thigh, extends back behind the player, and ends up in an "L" position next to the head.

While the "long C" is important and should be used when possible, there are times when a different version of the "C" needs to be used by an infielder. While the "long C" is beneficial physically, it requires too much time in certain situations. The correct motion for a throw that requires a quick release is the "short C." The "short C" is very similar to the "long C," but the path of the arm is shorter, allowing the fielder to release the ball faster. This throw is typically used when turning a double play, trying to recover from a fielding miscue, or charging a slow ground ball. Instead of the throwing hand grazing the thigh, as in the "long C," the "short C" requires the throwing hand to travel across the chest. The ball travels across the chest and forms a quick, short motion that resembles the letter "C." The ball does not need to extend completely back behind the player as discussed in chapter 3. The purpose of the "short C" is to release the ball quickly. It is important to remember that the "short C" motion, done repetitively and exclusively, will have an adverse effect on the elbow. It should only be done when necessary. Throwing with the "short C" on occasion will not create arm problems in a young player. However, if the "short C" is used exclusively, players can develop serious arm problems. For that reason, the "long C" technique should be favored in most circumstances.

Backhands and Forehands

The ball is rarely hit directly at an infielder. When balls are hit hard to the left or right of a player, a backhand or forehand technique is used to catch the ball. Both techniques need proper footwork. In the explanations below, a right-handed shortstop is assumed as the fielder.

 *See Section 6.12*

First Step

Whether the ball is fielded forehand or backhand, it is imperative that the fielder take a good first step. Just as important as the first step is the path the fielder takes to the ball. An infielder who can cover a lot of ground is said to have "good range." With the fielder's feet shoulder-width apart as the pitch arrives at the batter, the fielder's first step can be the difference between a base hit or an out. The quickest movement with the feet is a "cross-over step." A sharply ball hit ball to the player's right requires the fielder to take a hard, long step with the left foot to the right side. Most fielders initially take a small step with their right foot first. This step wastes time and covers little ground. The cross-over step is superior in helping the fielder move towards a ball to her right.  *See Section 6.12* The right foot crossing over the left is how a left-handed fielder will take the first step.

The first step enables the fielder to get to the ball faster. If the ball is hit hard and farther away from the fielder, the first step needs to be taken on a path behind the fielder. Using the right-handed shortstop example, the left foot would land behind the right so the path of the fielder would be deeper in order to get to the ball. If the ball is hit slower, the left foot would land in front of the right and the path would be toward the third baseman. The path taken is based on the speed of the ball and the distance the ball is from the fielder.

Backhand

Figure 6.3 *Backhand.*

A backhand refers to the position of the glove hand when the ball is hit to the right of a fielder (again, we are using a right-handed shortstop). As the fielder arrives to make the play, the ball should be fielded off the right foot. It is important to field the ball off the right foot, so the player can plant that foot and throw to the base without taking a wasted step. What if the ball cannot be caught off the right foot? The left is still an option. When fielding off of the left foot, the next step needs to be a plant with the right foot and a throw. The key to making an out is to eliminate any wasted steps that will give the baserunner more time. Fielding the ball off the right foot eliminates one step, which could be the difference between an out and a base hit.

During the backhand catch, the right foot should be bent when the ball is fielded. For a backhand catch, the glove is on the right side of the fielder's body. To catch the ball, the glove hand (the left hand in our example) is turned or rotated so that the front of the glove can face the ball. The right hand should still be positioned next to the glove for a quick transfer of the ball and a speedy release.

 *See Section 6.14*

Forehand

The forehand refers to a ball fielded on the left side of a right-handed fielder. The ball is fielded off the left foot, but can be fielded off the right foot. Once the ball is fielded, the player needs to rotate the body into a good throwing position. Many players rotate the body, but forget to line up the scope toward the intended target. The rotation needs to be quick and in one motion to save time.

 *See Section 6.15*

Covering the Bag at Second on a Steal

Fielding includes covering the bag at second base when a runner is stealing from first. Many players cover the base incorrectly. Safety and effectiveness are the two main concerns for teaching the correct way to cover a base on steal attempts.

Many players straddle the base when a runner attempts to steal from first. "Straddling the base" refers to the fielder standing directly over the base with the right and left foot on either side. This technique is not recommended. A player stealing from first will normally slide into second base. With the player straddling the bag, the fielder is directly in line with the sliding player's feet and spikes. Avoiding these spikes is possible if the player does not straddle the bag.

Another problem with straddling the bag is fielding the throw from the catcher. If the ball is thrown from the catcher on the first base side, the player may needs to come off the bag. In this instance the fielder is attempting to catch the ball in the same path as the runner. When a catcher throws the ball to second, especially in youth baseball, a low throw is probable. Most young arms have trouble reaching the base with the throw. A short hop makes the throw even more difficult, especially when the fielder is straddling the bag.

A better way to cover the bag is this. Instead of straddling the bag, the player stands in front of second base. The left foot should be on the front corner of the base (the corner pointing toward the pitcher). This allows the fielder to do many more positive things. First, it places the fielder out of the direct path of the runner. Second, it puts the player in a better position to handle a low throw, since he or she is closer to the catcher. Finally, an errant throw to the first-base side of the base allows the fielder to come off the base and out of the way of the runner. The ball can be caught without a collision. The tag can still be made with the left foot on the front corner. When the ball arrives, simply bend the left leg and swipe the glove across the front of the base to make the play. The fielder can also reach the back corner of the base if the runner decides to slide to avoid the tag.

It is important to make a quick, deliberate tag when making the out. Do not put the glove on the ground and allow the runner to slide into it. The ball has a good chance of being kicked out of the glove, and there is a chance the fielder's hand could be injured by a runner sliding hard into the base. Apply the tag quickly and get the glove out of harm's way.

Relays from the Outfield

When a ball is hit to the outfield, the exchange from outfielder to infielder is important for preventing runners from advancing. The throw is called a *relay throw*, and the player catching the ball from the outfield and throwing it to second, third, or home is called the *relay man* or *cutoff*. While the idea seems fairly simple, many games are lost because teams can't execute relay throws quickly and efficiently.

Who is the Relay, or Cutoff Man?

 *See Section 6.16*

Eliminating confusion on who is the relay man on a ball hit to the outfield is important. Every player has a job on a ball hit to the outfield. To alleviate confusion, the relay man (the person receiving the ball from the outfield) should be predetermined.

Determining who is the cutoff depends on two aspects of the situation: where in the outfield the ball is hit, and the base (or home plate) to which it is going to be thrown. It will be thrown to the base where the fielders believe the runner can be thrown out, that is, where a play can be made.

If the relay man is throwing the ball to second base, the general rule of thumb is that on a ball hit to right field, the second baseman is the relay. On a ball hit to left field, the shortstop is the relay.

If the throw is supposed to go to third base, the shortstop is always the relay person no matter where the ball is hit to the outfield. The second baseman's job is to cover second base.

When the relay throw is intended for home plate, the responsibilities change. On a ball hit to right field or center field, the first baseman is the cutoff. A ball hit to left field is the responsibility of the third baseman. The shortstop will cover third as the runner rounds third base, and the second baseman will cover second base.

In a situation where a ball is hit deep to the outfield, a double cutoff may be needed. The throw from the outfield fence is very far for the outfielder. If the ball is hit to left field and the throw needs to go home, the shortstop may have to go out between the third baseman and the outfielder to reduce the distance. The opposite holds true for a ball hit to the right field fence. The second baseman may have to go out and close the distance between the first baseman and the right fielder.

In all instances above, each player's responsibility in a given situation should be rehearsed in practice, so there is no confusion during games. Infielders should know what positions to occupy when the ball is hit past the infield. Communication is important in these cases, because the ball is in play and one or more runners are in motion.

The Relay Person

The player must catch the ball (from a player in the outfield) and make an accurate throw to the intended target. If the catch or throw does not occur swiftly, the relay will break down and the opponent will score runs.

The relay person can improve the chances of a successful exchange. When the relay person gets into position, his or her hands should go up and a verbal cue should be yelled, so the outfielder can identify the target. As the ball arrives, the relay person should line up the body so the ball is caught and then thrown in a continuous motion. The throwing arm should be pointed toward the outfielder. With the throwing side angled toward the outfielder, the scope will already be aligned with the intended target. As the ball is handled by the relay person, it should appear as if the ball never stops. A good relay is quick and accurate. The ball is thrown to the relay person, and the relay person immediately throws the ball to the target.

Summary

Fielding a baseball requires quick feet, sound fundamentals, and a positive attitude. As much as becoming a good hitter demands hours of practice swings, becoming a good infielder takes practice fielding ground balls. The more ground balls a player can field, the more comfortable it becomes during a game.

CHAPTER 7

Turning the Double Play

THE home run is the most exciting offensive play in baseball. If a defensive play was chosen to be the most exhilarating, it would have to be the double play. A double play fashions two outs from one batted ball, and stifles the offense. The traditional double play occurs with a runner on first base and a ground ball hit to one of the infield positions. A fielder with the ball steps on or throws to second base before the runner from first arrives to force one out, and then fires the ball to the first baseman to force out the batter for the second out.

There are other, less conventional ways to turn a double play. A line drive or fly ball can be caught for the first out, and the player catching the ball throws to a base where a runner is caught off the base before being able to tag up. With runners on first and second, or the bases loaded, there are many ways a team can turn a double play.

In this chapter, the traditional double play is presented and techniques described to help execute the play with speed and accuracy. The double play will be presented in terms of each infield position. However, the main focus will be on the shortstop and second baseman. The end of the chapter offers drills to help improve a player's effectiveness.

This symbol indicates reference to Companion DVD for video instruction

Shortstop

The shortstop is arguably the most important position player when turning a double play. The shortstop position is often played by the individual with the strongest arm and quickest feet and hands.

In most cases, the shortstop is the player that needs to be involved in order to ensure that two outs are made.

Fielding a Double Play Ball (Shortstop)

For fielding a double play ball, the technique used is a little different from the conventional fielding technique (see Chapter 6 for the conventional fielding technique). Turning a double play requires speed and precision. The primary objective is to catch the ball quickly and deliver the ball to second base as accurately as possible.

Figure 7.1 *Turning the double play.*

See Section 7.1

Positioning is important when setting up for a double play. Playing too deep in the infield or too far from second base does not give the shortstop enough time to complete the double play. The shortstop needs to shift or "cheat" a little toward second base, while at the same time taking a few steps in toward the hitter. This positioning enables the shortstop to throw to, or run to, second base more quickly.

See Section 7.2

A ball hard hit right at the shortstop is basic. The fielder must get the feet into a stable fielding position to make a good throw without taking any unnecessary steps. Once the the ball is caught, the fielder shifts his or her weight to the right foot and makes a quick throw to second base. Many players tend to stand up and shuffle the feet before throwing, which wastes valuable time. The key is not to stand up but to stay low when throwing the ball to the second baseman. The second baseman's contribution is also crucial. He must catch the throw from the shortstop, turn, and throw accurately to first—while avoiding the sliding runner.

For the double play, a ball hit to the shortstop's left is ideal. The shortstop moves to the left, fields the ball, and keeps moving toward second base. While staying low, the shortstop flips the ball, with no arc on it, to the second baseman. The glove should be moved out of the way when flipping, so the second baseman can see the ball from the time it is tossed. The shortstop should put the glove on the glove-side hip to avoid impeding the view of the second baseman. It is important that the shortstop keep moving toward second base, even after the ball is released. This will ensure the flip has no arc.

 See Section 7.3

The ball hit to the right of the shortstop is a more difficult play, since the shortstsop's momentum is shifting away from second base. When possible, the fielder needs to face and be lined up with the oncoming baseball, plant the feet, and make a hard throw to second base. If it is not possible to have the ball lined up in front, the player should realize that the first task is just to catch the ball and make at least one out. When the ball is very far to the shortstop's right, the backhand catch will have to be used (see Chapter 6 for the backhand technique). Here the shortstop should make the throw that's easier from the position she's in, either to second base or first.

See Section 7.4

A slow roller to the shortstop is also a tough ball on which to turn a double play. As with the ball hit to the shortstop's right, the primary objective is to get at least one out. If the throw to second presents itself, it should be accurate. However, a throw on the run is often difficult to make accurately. There is a good chance that turning a double play will not be an option, and the easier out should be made, which is to force the batter by throwing to first.

Remember, a successful "single play" (one sure out) is better than a failed double play, where zero outs are recorded.

Feeding the Second Baseman

"Feeding" refers to throwing the ball to the second baseman at a location that makes it as easy as possible to make the next throw. When feeding the second baseman from the shortstop position, ask the second baseman where he or she likes the ball. The optimal feed is different for each and every player. The second baseman should show the shortstop where the ball should be placed in order to make the play.

When making the feed to second, the throw should be crisp and without an arc, but not too hard. The idea is to throw a ball that is easy to handle by the second baseman. Poor throws from the shortstop make it difficult for the second baseman to catch and deliver the ball to first.

Second Baseman   If the shortstop is the most important key to turning a double play, the second baseman is not far behind. The traditional double play is handled by both the shortstop and second baseman at some point, so the second baseman needs to possess strong fundamentals.

Fielding a Double Play Ball (Second Baseman)

As in the case of the shortstop, the second baseman is positioned differently when anticipating a double play ball. Normally the second baseman has more time than a shortstop to field a ball and throw to first, because of his proximity to first base. On a double play ball, the second baseman must field and throw the ball more quickly than he or she normally does.

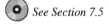 *See Section 7.5*

The depth of the positioning again is important. Playing too deep in the infield or too far from second does not give the second baseman enough time to complete the double play. The second baseman must also move or cheat a little toward second base and take a few steps in toward the hitter.

 *See Section 7.6*

On a hard ball hit directly at him, the second baseman needs to break down into a good fielding position (see Chapter 6 for the mechanics of a good fielding position). After fielding the ball, he simply rotates the body so his leading shoulder or "scope" is in line with second base and then delivers a crisp throw to the

Figure 7.2 *Turning the double play to the left.*

shortstop. It is important that the player does not stand up and take unnecessary steps toward second base when throwing the ball. Some players like to swivel on the left foot and to place their left knee on the ground when feeding the ball to the shortstop. This technique can be effective, but must feel comfortable to the player. If it does not, the swivel can still occur and the left leg stays bent during the throw without the knee touching the ground. To make an accurate throw to the shortstop at second base, it is important to line up the lead shoulder.

A ball hit to the right of the second baseman is the ideal ground  *See Section 7.7* ball for turning the double play. The second baseman catches the ball and continues toward second base. In this situation, instead of throwing the ball, the second baseman flips the ball to the shortstop without arc. It is important for the second baseman to continue moving even after the ball is flipped toward second. This will keeps the ball moving fast and eliminates the arc. The glove should be pulled out of the way by placing it on the left hip, so the shortstop can see the ball clearly. The second baseman should bear to the right after flipping the ball, in effect veering away in order to avoid the shortstop and the runner.

Ground balls to the left of the second baseman are difficult  *See Section 7.8* double-play opportunities. The second baseman needs to decide whether to go to first base for one out, or second base to try to turn the double play. The decision should be made based on the speed of the batted ball and the baserunner's speed. On a decision to go to second base with the ball, the second baseman needs to field the ball off the left foot, turn his or her back toward home plate, plant the right foot, and throw the ball to second. The movement will spin the player almost completely around. When the right foot plants, make sure the lead shoulder, or "scope," is pointing toward

Figure 7.3 *Lining up the scope.*

second. This move takes a lot of practice and needs to be rehearsed until mastered. When done correctly, it is the fastest way to turn a double play on a ball hit to the left of the second baseman.

On a slow roller, it is very difficult to turn a double play. The best choice is to get an out at first base and avoid attempting the double play.

Feeding the Shortstop

The techniques for feeding the shortstop are virtually the same as for feeding the second baseman, as described above. Different players prefer different feeds, and the second baseman and shortstop must both understand and practice the feeds that suit them best.

First and Third Base

Turning the double play from the first or third base position requires the fielder to release the ball very quickly to the pivot man at second. After fielding the ball, the player needs to take a quick shuffle of the feet or no step at all depending on the strength of the player's arm. The first and third baseman should ask the shortstop and second baseman where they like to receive the ball when turning a double play. The ball needs to be thrown accurately and fast to that spot using a four-seam grip when possible.

If the first baseman fields the ball close to first base, the first base bag should be stepped on before the throw is made to second. After touching first, the first baseman must alert the shortstop at second. In this situation, the shortstop needs to apply a tag to the runner moving from first to second because the force play has been eliminated. A "force play" refers to when a runner must advance to the next base because there is a runner behind him ready to occupy the base he held. In the case above, the runner is "forced" to run to second base because the batter needs to occupy first. In the play described here, the first baseman has already stepped on first, and the batter is out. Since there is no runner be-hind him, the runner moving to second base is no longer forced. To be out, the runner must be tagged. Telling the shortstop with a verbal cue of some kind reminds the player to apply a tag.

Footwork is critical for either shortstop or second baseman while taking a feed at second and preparing to throw to first. As the ball arrives at second base, the transfer to first must be swift.

Taking the Feed at Second Base

Shortstop

The shortstop is the player making the play at second base on a ground ball to second or first base. Most of the time the shortstop will be the player covering second on a bunted ball, or hit back to the pitcher. The second baseman could cover on the ball bunted or back to the pitcher, but the idea is to have the shortstop cover the bag because of the shortstop's strong arm and momentum going toward first base.

Before the ball is received by the shortstop, good footwork plays a vital role in helping relay the ball quickly to first base. Instead of standing on the base and waiting for the ball to arrive, the shortstop needs to keep the feet moving and stay behind the base. As the ball is thrown towards second, the player must work through the baseball. "Working through the baseball" refers to moving toward the baseball as it is thrown and continuing that motion even after catching the ball. After working through the ball, the player drags the right foot across the base, plants the same foot on the ground, and throws to first. The steps should be quick and short. The idea is to catch the ball and get rid of it as quickly as possible. Working through the ball is a key element in turning the double play quickly. It allows the shortstop to make a harder throw to first base. The shortstop and ball should arrive at second base at the same time. After completing the throw, the shortstop should be on the first base side of second base.

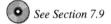 *See Section 7.9*

Another reason for staying behind the base and keeping the feet moving is in case the feed is bad, i.e., the throw is off target. With the feet in motion, the shortstop has time to adjust to the ball's path to second base on any type of throw. If the player is standing still on the base, the only throw the shortstop can handle with good fundamentals is the ball thrown perfectly.

Working through the baseball also provides the momentum for a hard throw, but quick hands are another key component. It is important to have both hands together when catching the ball. With the throwing hand following the ball into the glove, the shortstop can quickly transfer the ball to the throwing hand and deliver an accurate throw to first base. The hands need to be quick, and the transfer of the ball from glove to hand swift. This action increases the chances of completing the double play.

Second Baseman

 *See Section 7.10*

With regard to the feed, the second baseman needs to take a different approach to turning the double play. As in the case of the shortstop, the second baseman should not stand on the bag and wait for the throw. The feet should be moving constantly before the feed, and the player should be behind the bag. As the ball is thrown, the second baseman makes the adjustment according to the throw. If the ball is thrown a little to the right, the second baseman goes to the right of the bag and vice verse for the ball thrown to the left of the base. Setting up behind the bag and keeping the feet moving enables the second baseman to react to the ball.

See Section 7.11

One difference between the second baseman and shortstop is momentum. The shortstop continues moving through second base and throws to first. On the other hand, the second baseman, who is looking away from first base, has to re-position herself to make a throw in the opposite direction. If the ball is thrown from the first base side of second, the player can use the base to push off with the right foot to make a throw to first. To increase quickness, the second baseman starts the footwork as the ball is arriving. The footwork should be a quick right-left throw to first using the base as a springboard. On a feed from the shortstop side of second base, the player needs to adjust the feet and step on the base with the left foot, propel the weight back onto the right foot, and push off with an accurate throw to first base. While the options vary according to where the feet plant or touch the base, the footwork should always be quick and never exceed more than two quick steps before the throw to first is made.

Tips and Drills for Turning the Double Play

Ozzie Smith or Omar Visquel (both great shortstops) would tell you that turning a double play well isn't a gift they were born with. Turning a double play requires practice, and more practice, and then a little more practice. Here are a number of drills that can make players better at turning the double play.

Soft Hands

 *See Section 7.12*

A great tool for developing quick hands, which are essential for delivering the ball quickly, is the soft hands device. This tool is a paddle or foam pad with finger inserts that mimics a glove. While on the glove hand, the device teaches a player how to use both hands when catching a ball. Using the soft hands creates a quick transfer from the glove to the throwing hand. If two hands are not used with this tool, the ball cannot be caught. The shortstop and second baseman can put on this tool and practice turning the double play. It will increase speed and eliminate wasted time. Once the "regular" glove is back on, the player more readily places the hands in the proper positions.

Double Play Team Drill

 *See Section 7.13*

If I were to rate drills on a scale from 1 to 10, this one would get an 11. The drill requires a third baseman, shortstop, second baseman, and first baseman. The players begin from their normal positions. The object of the drill is to practice the double play starting from each of the four infield positions.

The third baseman and shortstop are given a ball to begin. The third baseman pretends to field a grounder, and throws the ball to second. The second baseman turns the double play by throwing to first base. The first baseman drops the ball after catching it.

The shortstop then immediately flips or throws the ball to the second baseman who again throws it to first. As the first baseman receives the ball, the second baseman returns to his or her normal position, and the first baseman throws the ball to him or her.

The second baseman then pretends to field a ground ball and flips or throws the ball to the shortstop. The shortstop throws the ball to first base to complete the double play.

Finally, the first baseman pretends to field a ground ball and throws to the shortstop, who completes the double play by throwing back to first. After receiving the baseball, the first baseman throws the ball to the third baseman. The first baseman then picks up the other ball on the ground and throws it to the shortstop. The drill starts over again with the third baseman pretending to field a ground ball and starting a double play.

Teaching Tip

This drill can be done between innings during a game. Instead of the traditional method of the first baseman rolling ground balls to the fielders, the shortstop and third baseman can return to the field with a ball in their hand and practice turning two. It is a great way to work on the double play, and it will really baffle the opposing team.

This drill should be done quickly, with the ball moving constantly. When the players get the hang of the drill, it runs smoothly. The ball never touches the ground (other than the first baseman dropping the first ball), and the drill is great for practicing good throws when turning the double play.

 *See Section 7.14*

Four Corner Flip Drill

The four corner flip drill is designed especially for middle infielders (shortstops and second basemen). The drill requires five players. Four players should stand evenly apart to form a square, with each player at a corner of the square. The fifth person stands behind the person who's holding the ball and who starts the drill. Basically, the drill involves flipping the ball in one direction around the square with each throwing player moving into the position of the player to whom he or she is flipping in a continuing sequence.

The player with the ball begins by flipping the ball in either direction to the player next to him or her. During the flip, the glove should be tucked on the glove-side hip so the ball is in full view of the person receiving it. As the player flips the ball, he or she should continue moving toward the player receiving the ball. The player receiving the ball then flips it to the person next to him. The player who started the drill replaces, i.e., moves to, the position of the player who received the ball initially. This second player in turn tosses the ball and moves to the position of the third, and so on. After flipping the ball, each player takes the position of the person who receives the ball in a continuing series of flips and catches around the square. The fifth person jumps in to replace the person starting the drill, while the last person to receive the ball jumps out and becomes the new fifth person.

Teaching Tip

When practicing turning the double play with your middle infielders, don't just hit balls from home plate. Stand between the pitcher's mound and second base, and roll the ball to the desired spot on the field. This positioning allows the coach to direct the ball better. When a coach hits the ball from home plate, it is difficult to place the ball to cover the various scenarios. The positioning behind the pitcher's mound controls the situation better and allows for more repetitions. It also keeps the coach close to the infielders, so she can demonstrate the proper technique when needed.

Summary

Turning the double play can be taught to players of all ages. When taking an unofficial poll at coaching clinics, most coaches admit their team does not turn a single "traditional" double play during a season. With a little instruction and a great deal of practice, turning the double play can be a defensive weapon.

CHAPTER 8

Outfield Play

PLAYING the outfield is one of the more underrated roles on the diamond. Many believe outfielders simply need to catch fly balls. Catching the fly ball is just the beginning. A ball hit to the outfield needs to be played in just the right way, or the batter (and other runners) will be afforded the opportunity to advance. Often in a game and especially in youth leagues, once a ball leaves the infield, the chances of scoring are greatly increased, as are the chances for mistakes, such as missed balls, panicky throws, and even collisions. To catch the ball and quickly return a throw to the infield require good footwork, a strong arm, and the ability to read the ball off the hitter's bat. These outfielding basics are explained in this chapter.

Catching a fly ball is not a routine matter. Here, we break it down into the fundamentals.

Catching a Fly Ball

Ready Position

 *See Section 8.1*

Positioning is of great importance in outfield play. When the ball is hit, the outfielder needs to be in a "ready position." As the ball approaches home plate from the pitcher, the outfielder needs to be preparing to pursue the ball. Taking a few steps toward the plate and getting the feet in motion are the best ways to get a jump on the ball. The hands should not be on the knees and the fielder

This symbol indicates reference to Companion DVD for video instruction

should not be standing upright. The hands should be relaxed, positioned somewhere near the waist and in front of the body. The knees should be bent a little, and the player should be moving on every pitch.

Breaking on the Pitch and Footwork

A fly ball hit directly at an outfielder is routine. It is the ball hit in the gap or considerably away from the outfielder that presents a challenge. To run to the ball, the fielder needs to get a jump on the ball and use proper footwork. The time to practice reading the ball off of a player's bat is during batting practice. After tracking many fly balls, outfielders can become skilled at knowing whether a ball is hit deep or is going to drop shallow. Learning to recognize the difference between the two types of fly balls enables the outfielder to break in or retreat.

When a decision on where the ball is going to land is made, footwork becomes very important. Footwork can be the difference between making an out and having the ball drop for extra bases. The footwork does not change regardless of the position played in the outfield.

A ball hit directly at the outfielder requires little or no footwork. Even a ball that appears headed straight for the fielder can curve in the air. The rule of thumb on the motion of fly balls is this. The ball hit by a right-handed batter will have a tendency to curve or tail to the left of an outfielder. The ball may appear to be hit right at an outfielder, and sometimes that is the case, but the player should realize that fly balls off the bat of a right-handed hitter often tail to the left. If a left-handed batter is hitting, the ball will tail to the right of an outfielder. Outfielders should always be prepared for the ball to drift one way or the other.

 *See Section 8.2*
If the ball is hit to the left of the outfielder, a crossover step needs to be used in order to get to the ball quickly. A crossover step on a ball hit to the left side of the player is a "right over left" step. When the ball is hit to the outfielder's left, the fielder's first step needs to be with the right foot. The right foot crosses over the left allowing the outfielder to get a better jump on the ball. If the left foot were to take a step first, it would be a small step and not cover the ground like a crossover step.

 *See Section 8.3*
The opposite is true for a ball hit to the right of an outfielder.

Fly Ball Communication

The first step should be a "left over right" crossover step. Again, crossover steps are used for balls hit far enough away that the fielder must run to make the catch.

On a ball hit over an outfielder's head, the footwork changes. The crossover step needs to be a little deeper, or more in back of the player. The ball hit directly over the head of an outfielder poses the biggest challenge. If the hitter is right-handed, the outfielder needs to turn to the left. If it is a left-handed hitter, the outfielder should turn to the right. Observing the hitter prior to the ball being hit allows the player to react accordingly once the ball is in flight.

See Section 8.4

Using Two Hands

There is not a player or coach alive who has not heard the importance of using two hands when catching a ball. The throwing hand needs to follow the ball into the glove to prevent the ball from popping out. Not only does it eliminate dropped balls, but it allows a quick transfer of the ball from the glove to the throwing hand. When a runner on base tries to take an extra base after a ball is caught, the quick transfer from glove to hand helps the outfielder get ready for the throw.

See Section 8.5

There is a scenario that requires an outfielder to use only the glove hand to catch a fly ball without the throwing hand covering. If the outfielder is sprinting to track down a fly ball, only the glove hand should be used. It is very difficult, on a fast sprint, to reach up with the throwing hand and trap the ball in the glove. Using just the glove hand allows the throwing arm to continue the running motion, and the player can get more extension. Whenever possible, the throwing hand should try to cover the ball. Whether to use one or both hands will depend on the situation and requires judgment.

See Section 8.6

Catching a fly ball is a team activity. Regardless of the position played on the field, a fly ball requires *all* players on and off the field to communicate. When a ball is hit into the air, one fielder needs to take charge and be decisive. The rest of the players on the field and in the dugout help to guide the player as he or she prepares to catch the ball.

Fly Ball Communication

> **Teaching Tip**
>
> Have players face the coach and then turn and run on command. Toss a ball so the player must catch it "over the shoulder," with his or her back still turned. Make sure to lead the player, so the ball is caught on the run and the player uses one hand. The drill resembles a wide receiver and quarterback working on passing routes in football.

Chain of Command

There is an unwritten chain of command when a fly ball or pop up is in the air. All infielders let an outfielder catch the ball if he or she calls for it. If the shortstop calls for the ball and so does the left fielder, the shortstop lets the left fielder have the ball. In the outfield, the center fielder has the "right of way." If the center fielder calls for the ball, the left and right fielder should yield and let the centerfielder have the ball. In the infield, the middle infielders (shortstop and second) should take the ball when more than one player tries to catch it. If both middle infielders call for the ball, the shortstop takes control. The third and first baseman should always call off the pitcher and catcher. They are responsible for trying to catch a fly ball near home plate if possible. This fly ball chain of command greatly reduces the chance of collisions or dropped balls.

 *See Section 8.7*

Language

The traditional "I got it" and "You got it" or "Take it" are options when calling for a ball or confirming which player should catch it. However, there's a better way to communicate that will avoid confusion.

"I got it," "You got it," and "Take it" all contain the word "it" in the command. When a group of adrenaline-filled people are yelling, a fielder can easily be confused as the words get slurred together to sound like the same thing. Instead of having the player yell "I got it," using the word "ball" is a better option. It is one word and cannot be confused with any other baseball command. The rest of the team should be yelling "Take it" or the player's name. Unless the player's name is Saul, Paul, or something rhyming with "ball," the player has no doubt whether he or she is responsible for catching the ball. The rest of the players on the field should give the player room to make the catch.

If a ball becomes lost in the sun, or the player who called for the ball can no longer track it in the air, the command of "help" should be used. This command alerts the other players to the fact that the ball is lost and another fielder must take charge. Depending on angles or the sun, a player might need help after calling for the ball. The new player who takes command should yell "ball," and the player who shouted "help" should yield to the new player. The rest of the team yells the new player's name, so there is no confusion and the play can be made.

Outfielders need to be able to field ground balls. How the outfielder reacts to the ground ball depends in part on the situation. With some groundballs, such as clean base hits with no one on base, there is no chance to make an out. Often, however, outfielders must catch ground balls and throw them quickly to a base or to a cutoff person.

Ground Balls to the Outfield

When there is no chance to make an out, the outfielder needs to break down and make sure the ball stays in front of him or her. This situation usually occurs when a hitter strokes a single to the outfield, or a ball is hit directly at the outfielder and the runners are most likely not going to advance. The outfielder must lower the tailgate (the buttocks) and get the body in front of the baseball. A bobbled ball or one that gets by the outfielder allows the runners to move up a base and can prove costly. Some outfielders put a knee on the ground to make sure the ball stays in front.

 *See Section 8.8*

The other scenario requires the outfielder to field the ball and make a strong throw to a base. Unless the fielder is fairly close to the base the outfielder should always throw the ball to the cutoff person. The cutoff person or relay will have his or her hands in the air and be standing on the outfield grass. When fielding the ball, the outfielder needs to be moving toward the infield. The ball should be fielded on the run toward the glove-side of the body. As the ball is fielded, the player needs to perform a "crow hop." For a right-handed player, a crow hop is a "right foot-left foot" jump in the air that propels the fielder forward. A "left foot-right foot" jump would be used for a left-handed player. It is important to understand that the hop is not a jump directly up in the air. The hop should be a jump toward the infield. The idea is to generate a lot of

 *See Section 8.9*

momentum toward the infield to make a strong throw. The crow hop will generate more hip speed, producing a stronger throw to the desired base.

Teaching Tip

The crow hop can be taught using a cone or other small object. Roll ground balls or toss fly balls to the outfielder behind the cone. The player must catch the ball and bound over the obstruction. Make sure the obstacle is not so tall that it encourages jumping straight up into the air.

Throwing from the Outfield

Throwing properly is a key part of playing the outfield. Even if a ball is fielded cleanly, a poor throw might equate to runs for the other team, or runner(s) advancing to the next base and closer to scoring. Good fundamentals when throwing need to be used to avoid a big inning from the opposition.

The basics of throwing from the outfield are identical to those discussed in Chapter 3. Lining up the scope, gripping the ball with four seams, and using the legs all contribute to a strong and accurate throw.

One misconception players have is that a ball must be thrown on the fly to the target base or to home plate. More important is that the ball should be thrown accurately to the cutoff person. If the cutoff person is not needed, the ball can be thrown on a hop to the desired base. Infielders will admit that a ball on a hop is just as easy to field, if not easier, than catching a ball in the air. Trying to throw the ball on the fly to a base often leads to an overthrow. The important concept to learn is to throw the ball on a direct line to the base.

Balls at the Fence

See Section 8.10

When a ball is hit to a fence, whether it is in the outfield or in foul ground, it is important to find the fence first before fielding the ball. Many players will go after the ball tentatively, reaching for the ball at the last second because of the fear of colliding with the fence. When the ball is in the air near the fence, make sure to run to the fence first and understand where the fence is in relation to the body. Then concentrate on catching the ball. This sequence allows the outfielder to make the out, and more importantly, avoid a collision with the fence.

Teaching Tip

Catching balls at the fence should be practiced. The player is positioned so that he or she must retreat towards the fence. The coach tosses balls that lead the player towards the fence. The player is instructed to get a sense of the fence first, and then catch the ball.

Summary

An outfielder has a lot of responsibility during a game. One reason for this is that often the outfielder catches balls that are hits, and thus is frequently in a situation where one or more runners are advancing. Another reason is that fly balls to the outfield, if not handled properly, can permit—or at least tempt—runners to take an extra base. While infielders are more active during a game, the outfielder's chances are even more important when they present themselves. By applying fundamentals, the outfielder can improve and become a valuable asset to a team. Throwing advancing runners out and tracking down possible extra base hits make an outfielder's defense a team's best offense.

CHAPTER 9

12 Defensive Drills and Games for Infielders and Outfielders

DEFENSIVE basics for both infielding and outfielding can be learned through games and drills. Although there are too many to mention in one chapter, here are a few of the more popular drills and games for younger players. They've been selected with two ideas in mind: fun and effectiveness.

Soft Hands

The soft hands tool was described earlier. Using the soft hands creates a quick transfer from the glove to the throwing hand. If two hands are not used with the soft hands mitt, the ball cannot be caught. The soft hands can be used to replace the glove for any drill at any position.

Quick Hands

The quick hands drill requires two players. The players should be approximately twenty-five feet apart. The object is to move the ball back and forth between the players as quickly as possible. One of the players starts the drill by throwing to the other. The exchange goes back and forth between the players. Throwing the ball accurately and transferring the ball from the glove to the throwing hand needs to be swift. To make this drill more advanced, have the players use a soft hands tool.

Infield Drills

 *See Section 9.1*

 *See Section 9.2*

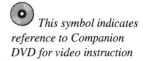 *This symbol indicates reference to Companion DVD for video instruction*

> ### Teaching Tip
>
> The quick hands drill can be chaotic. The players try to rush the throw, and inaccuracy becomes a problem. Have the players begin this drill by throwing slowly and working their way into a faster tempo. The footwork and ball transfer from glove to hand are the key elements to a successful exchange. The throw needs to be accurate in order to be beneficial to both players.

 *See Section 9.3*

Pick-ups

In pick-ups, two players face one another about five feet apart. One player is on one knee and is called the feeder. The other player faces the feeder in a good fielding position. The feeder has two baseballs. The feeder rolls one ball to either the right or left of the fielder, so the fielder has to slide the feet (without crossing over) to field the ball. As the player fields the ball, he or she flips it back to the feeder. As the ball is flipped, the feeder rolls the second ball to the other side. The process continues for a predetermined amount of time. This drill strengthens the legs and is good for rehearsing the correct fundamentals.

> ### Teaching Tip
>
> When conducting the pick-up drill, make sure the player keeps the tailgate lowered and uses good fielding fundamentals. Many times a player will get tired, and good technique is sacrificed. Avoid overdoing this drill.

 *See Section 9.4*

Short-hop Hockey

With two players facing one another about five feet apart, short-hop hockey reinforces the importance of getting the hands out in front of the body, lowering the tailgate, and looking the ball into the glove.

One of the two players starts with a ball. A glove is optional for this drill. The player with the ball gives a short hop right in front of the opposing player. The opposing player should already have the tailgate lowered and the arms extended in front of the body. The person throwing the ball throws the ball like a dart. The object is not to throw the ball hard but to place it under the glove so it goes through the other player's legs. If the tailgate is not lowered and the glove is not on the ground, the ball will get through the legs. The players can keep score and see who can "shoot" the most baseballs through the other's legs.

Four Corners

See Section 9.5

In four corners, four players stand evenly apart to form a square. Each player represents a corner of the square. The players should be approximately fifty feet apart, or stand on each base on the infield. One of the four players has a baseball and starts by throwing it to a player on either side. The object is to move the ball around the square as quickly as possible. The player receiving the ball keeps the ball moving in the same direction by throwing to the next person. If the players are standing on the bases, the ball would move from home, to first, then second, to third, and then back to home and continue around in the same direction again. Baseball players call this "throwing it around the horn."

Four corners is great for teaching players to throw the ball accurately and quickly. The coach can blow a whistle or give a verbal cue to have the players throw the ball in the opposite direction.

Stationary Ball Drill

See Section 9.6

All of the players on a team can do the stationary ball drill at once, but only one player is necessary for completing the activity. With a ball placed approximately ten feet away from the player on the ground, the fielder gets in a good ready position. When a verbal cue is given by the coach, the player fields the ball and freezes, just as he's ready to throw. The coach thus has a chance to look over the player's fundamentals while fielding the ball.

To really work on the fundamentals, a variation of this drill can be done. When the fielder gets to the ball, he or she should freeze. The coach can walk up and down a line of players and see if the correct fundamentals are being used. The coach should look for the arms extended, staggered feet, a lowered tailgate, the bead on the top of the cap (head down), and the weight on the balls of the feet. A verbal cue can be given for the player to pick up the ball and get into a throwing position. The coach should look for a four-seam grip, the scope lined up with the target, and check to see if the player has worked through the ball toward the target. Isolating these movements with this drill is a great way to reinforce the proper fielding fundamentals.

Outfield Drills

See Section 9.7

Quarterback Drill

The quarterback drill teaches outfielders to take a good route to the ball, and to communicate with other players.

With the coach pretending to be a quarterback, a player is positioned fifteen feet on either side facing the same direction. The players are set up like wide receivers in football. When the coach gives the signal, both players start running and the coach lofts a ball somewhere between the two. One of the players has to take control and yell for the ball while the second player yields and confirms verbally that the other should take it. After the play has been made, two more players step into the wide receiver position, and the drill continues.

See Section 9.8

Come-and-go Drill

Come-and-go is a good drill to teach players how to field a ground ball and fly ball in the same activity. This drill is great for teaching players to catch a ball on the run and over the head.

The coach rolls a ground ball to a player positioned twenty-five feet away. The player charges the ball and flips it to the coach. After flipping the ball, the player must turn and run as hard as he or she can. The coach then throws the ball over the player's head, so that the player must catch the ball in the air.

See Section 9.9

Three-man Relay

The three-man relay teaches outfielders to hit the cutoff person accurately. The drill is good for infielders too. If only a single infielder is included, he or she should be placed in the middle position.

The drill begins with three players standing in a straight line approximately fifty feet apart (more than three players can be used for this drill). The ball should be started at one of the ends. The player who has the ball takes a crow hop and throws to the middle player, who immediately throws to the third person in the line. When the third person receives the ball, the ball should be caught and immediately thrown back to the middle player, with the thrower using a crow hop. The middle player receives the ball and throws it back to the player who started the drill. Throwing the ball accurately and moving the ball quickly are the chief objectives of the three-man relay.

Teaching Tip

Teach players to move the feet before the ball is caught. Moving the feet allows a player to catch the ball and immediately return a throw to the next target. A little crow hop or shuffle of the feet as the ball arrives is the fastest way to catch and then return an accurate throw.

Chuck It in the Bucket

 *See Section 9.10*

Outfielders need to make an accurate throw to complete this drill successfully. This is a great game to play with your outfielders and rewards the player who throws the ball to the intended target accurately.

Place a bucket at home plate, or any other base. Stand in the outfield and throw the outfielder a fly ball or grounder. The player needs to field the ball and make an accurate throw so the ball lands in the bucket. The ball does not need to land in the bucket on the fly. The drill helps players practice throwing the ball online to the base. Missing the bucket by a foot or two would constitute a good throw.

Big Air Drill

See Section 9.11

The big air drill is a favorite. It works on a player's lateral movement and teaches quickness to the ball.

Five balls are placed in front of the coach, who's in the kneeling position. The player is approximately ten feet away facing the coach. The coach tosses a ball in the air to either the player's left or right. The player must get to the ball and touch it with the glove. The player does not need to catch the ball, just touch it. As soon as the ball is touched, the coach tosses another ball to the opposite side, so the player has to hustle to touch the ball. The next ball should be thrown to the opposite side until four balls are tossed. The fifth ball is called the "hero ball." This ball should be thrown farther away, so the player has to dive to touch it. It is amazing how far players can dive to reach a ball. A player learns to move the body faster the more the drill is done. A variation of this drill can be done to see how many balls the player can touch. The big air drill can be a contest among the players to see who can touch the most baseballs.

 *See Section 9.12*

Flip and Fly

Flip and fly is another drill for teaching players to catch the ball on the run. It requires two coaches, or a player and a coach directing the drill.

Two coaches need to stand back to back with about a five-foot space between them. The players are standing in two lines. One line is formed to the right of the coaches about thirty feet away, the other line to the left at the same distance. Each line should have approximately four balls to start, with the first four players holding the balls. The first player in each line begins to jog. One line jogs in front of one coach, the other line trots in front of the other coach. As the player arrives at the coach, the ball should be flipped to the coach and then the player starts to sprint, continuing in the same direction. The coach lofts a ball well in front of the player, who tries to catch the ball with one hand on the run. Make sure to lead the player, so the ball is caught on the run. After catching the ball, the player files to the back of the line in the other group. The caught ball is then handed to a player in front of the line. The next player starts to jog when the coach throws the ball. Players love to do this drill, which also can be used to improve conditioning.

Summary While all of the above drills are fun and effective, variations of the drills are always a possibility. The important concept is to make the drills fun, and at the same time have a specific skill in mind to teach the players.

CHAPTER 10

Pitching

THERE is no position on the field more important than the pitcher. Good pitching stops good hitting. An effective pitcher can dominate a game and is a hot commodity from youth leagues to the majors. No matter what level of play, a team will only advance as far as their pitching will take them.

The problem with pitching is not finding players with strong arms. The problem is finding pitchers who can throw strikes and keep their arm healthy. The most injured body parts in sports today are the throwing shoulder and elbow. How do we prevent such injuries, especially in the growing player? Preventing arm injuries involves two ingredients: teaching the fundamentals and not inflating a young player's pitch count. These two elements of pitching are often overlooked when coaching young pitchers. Poor mechanics and being left too long on the mound cause injury.

This chapter applies the K.I.S.S. method: "**K**eep **I**t **S**imple, **S**on." With all of the training tools and gadgets on the market to-day, people are always looking for ways to get an edge on the competition. The way to get an edge is to perfect the basics. A pitcher must keep it simple and work on the fundamentals in order to throw harder and develop a healthy arm.

This symbol indicates reference to Companion DVD for video instruction

Safety is the #1 concern when dealing with young pitchers. Players are developing arm injuries at an alarming rate. Before the age of thirteen, the arm is not fully developed, and putting stress on the arm creates problems that will show up as the player gets

Safety/Pitch Count

older. The emphasis should be on safety, not winning. Winning will come when the arm is cared for and the mechanics are perfected.

Stretching/warming Up

When players arrive at the field, the first thing they do is pick up a ball and start throwing. The correct way to loosen the arm is not by throwing the baseball. The player must stretch the arm and get it loose *before* picking up a baseball. Chapter 2 contains ways to stretch the arm and get it loose. The rotator cuff is a complex area comprising four tiny muscles. Throwing before stretching inflicts stress on that region. A routine must be established that involves stretching before a ball is thrown.

Icing the Arm

I recently heard a minor league player tell kids that they do not need to ice the arm after pitching. The comment was, "You are young. You don't need to ice the arm." I couldn't disagree more. With a young, tender, and impressionable arm, applying ice should be mandatory. The player is going to have inflammation in the arm after throwing the baseball hard. Icing doesn't need to occur immediately after pitching. However, on the way home or after arriving home the player should put some ice on the arm. The areas iced should be the shoulder and elbow. Keeping some ice on the arm for fifteen to twenty minutes is enough to reduce inflammation and prevent injury.

Teaching Tip

A great way to make sure players ice their arm is to freeze water in paper cups. Bring the frozen cups to a game and store them in a small cooler. When the game is over, peel off the bottom of the cup to expose the ice. The player can rub the ice cup over the shoulder and elbow to reduce inflammation.

Pitch Count

More and more leagues are developing a rule that prevents a

pitcher from throwing too many pitches in one outing. This is a great idea. Certain leagues have an "innings pitched" rule. The latter rule is practical, but it's not as good as the pitch count rule. A player can throw a lot of pitches in two or three innings, leading to a tired or weak arm. A pitch count should be established based on a player's age.

Pitch counts should be regulated and monitored by youth coaches. If a player is under the age of twelve, he or she should throw no more than fifty pitches in a game (eighty during a week). The limit of fifty applies to pitches thrown from the mound during a game—not to every throw by a player. If the pitcher is between the ages of thirteen and fifteen, a good limit is seventy-five pitches per game, or one hundred and twenty-five during a week. While these limits are estimates, erring on the low side is recommended. Regulating the number of pitches keeps a pitcher from developing arm fatigue, which can lead to poor mechanics. Throwing at home is not recommended on the same night a pitcher throws in a game. A player should rest his arm and should not be permitted to pitch on a day after throwing more than twenty-five pitches from the mound.

Pitching for more than one team in a given season is also not recommended. A young pitcher should pitch for a single team no longer than nine months in a given year. If one season ends and another begins during those nine months, then playing for two teams is possible. No matter what, the arm needs an extended period of time to rest. Practicing between outings is encouraged, with certain qualifications. The player needs to remember to throw slower and not as hard as during a game. The focus of practice should be on mechanics and pitch location.

Mechanics

To throw harder and keep the arm healthy, proper pitching mechanics must be learned and established. Last year I worked with a player who had poor pitching mechanics. When I tried to change the mechanics to make him more effective, his father stepped in and asked me not to change his technique. His reason? The boy threw hard and was getting kids out. The player was developing a little elbow soreness already . . . at ten years old! After I explained to the father that his son was going to develop arm problems at a later time, the father still wanted his son to throw with the flawed mechanics.

It is a shame that parents and coaches permit young arms to be ruined because of the "win now" attitude. At a young age, the emphasis should be on mechanics and safety. If the aforementioned parent would have let me alter his son's mechanics, the player would throw harder and possibly avoid a trip to the physical therapist. Do your players a favor. Teach the proper mechanics. The player may struggle with control and it might feel uncomfortable, but over time the player is going to develop into a healthy pitcher, and the soundness of the pitcher will translate into effective performance.

Here, pitching mechanics are going to be broken down into five phases. Each phase, when done correctly, will prevent injury and allow the pitcher to throw accurately and with more velocity.

 *See Section 10.1*

Phase I: The Grip

The best pitch in baseball is the strike. For players to throw strikes, controlling the baseball is important. The player should grip the ball with four seams (refer to Chapter 3 for the four-seam grip). When a player can throw the ball consistently for strikes with four seams, teaching the two-seam grip is in order. The two-seam grip (refer to Chapter 3) makes the ball move more, due to aerodynamics. The two-seam grip makes the pitched ball tougher to hit, but also can be difficult to control by the pitcher. The focus, regardless of the grip, should be to control the ball and throw to the desired location.

Inspired by professional baseball, a pitcher can end up on the disabled list with a blister on one of the throwing fingers. Finger blisters pop up because the ball is pitched with the finger tips across the raised seams. Done repeatedly, this action creates friction. A pitcher should not grip the baseball deep in the hand. The ball gripped deep in the hand resists leaving a pitcher's grip. In essence, the pitcher who grips the ball tightly loses velocity and throws an unwanted changeup. To get more velocity, the ball needs to be held in the hand loosely, as though you were holding an egg. A gap or open space should be formed between the ball and the palm of the hand.

Make sure to hold the ball with the thumb directly under the ball. Many pitchers grip the ball with the thumb on the side of the baseball. It is hard to control the ball with the thumb on the side. When the ball is released, the ball will veer to the right or left, depending on where the thumb is placed. If the thumb is directly under the baseball, the ball will be released toward the intended location.

Phase II: The Wind-up

 *See Section 10.2*

The wind-up has no purposes other than creating momentum and leading into the next phase of pitching. Nevertheless, a wind-up can be a detrimental phase, if the technique is not correct.

How should players set up and place their feet in relation to the pitching rubber? The criteria for standing on the rubber are the same for right-handed and left-handed pitchers. Where to stand on the rubber depends on the hitter at the plate. If the hitter is right-handed, the player should stand on the right side of the pitching rubber. If the hitter is left-handed, the left side should be chosen. Why? Let's put 6'10" Randy Johnson on the mound. With his unbelievable physical presence and lightning velocity, he is much more intimidating when standing directly in line with the batter. If he stood on the opposite side of the mound, his presence diminishes a little because his throwing motion doesn't have the illusion of coming right at the hitter. Standing on the same side as the hitter gives the illusion to the batter that the pitcher is throwing right at him.

When standing on the mound, the player's heels should rest on the pitching rubber. Many pitching mounds develop holes in front of the rubber. When a pitcher goes into the wind-up, the heel can slide into the hole instead of the foot stepping into it. Pitchers who place their toes on the pitching rubber have to step into the hole and can lose their balance, or worse, twisting an ankle.

If the pitcher is right-handed, the first step should be back with the left foot. The step shouldn't be directly behind the rubber, but to the left side and back. This step allows the pitcher to get into a good balanced position, which is the next (and most important) phase of the process. If the step is directly back, it is difficult to swing the left leg up and get into a balanced position on the mound. The opposite is true for the left hander. The left-hander's step should be to the right and back with the right foot.

While stepping back with the left foot (for a right-hander), the head should not follow the foot. The head should stay over top of the posting foot. The "posting foot" is the foot that slides in front of the rubber. Bringing the head back with the foot stepping back overloads the weight too far to one side. This overloading will be hard to compensate for when moving into the balanced position. The head should not move much, if at all.

With the left foot stepping back and to the left (for a right-handed pitcher), the right foot should pivot in front of the pitching rubber. Some players pivot on top of the rubber. This is not correct and should be clarified to the pitcher. The pitcher needs to be able to push with the right foot and drive toward home. If the right foot is on top of the rubber, it has nothing to push from and tends to slip.

When teaching the motion of the wind-up, make sure the pitcher's tempo is slow and controlled. Young pitchers think the faster the wind-up, the more velocity on the pitch. This is a misconception. If this were the case, throwing from the stretch position would reduce velocity, which it does not. The slow, controlled wind-up allows the pitcher to get into the next phase, the balance position.

See Section 10.3

Phase III: The Balance Position

The balance position is the most important phase in the pitching process. This position gets the body under control and directed toward home plate. The balance position must be taught and learned properly, since it is a key to pitching accurately and consistently.

For a right-handed pitcher, the left leg needs to be picked up in a slow, controlled motion. The legs should be in a position in which the player could rest a cup of water on the left leg without the water spilling. Raising the thigh parallel to the ground creates

Figure 10.1 *The balance position.*

more drive toward home plate in the next phase. When teaching a player to get into the balance position, make the player hold the position for a five count. If the player can hold the position for five seconds without wavering, a balance position has been achieved.

The raised leg should be kept closed, which means the knee of the raised leg should not be pointed toward home or toward second base. The knee (for a right-hander) should be pointed somewhere in the third base direction.

To maintain balance, the pitcher should keep the hands together on the thigh, or near the waist area. Keeping the hands in this location helps with balance, since this is the pitcher's center of gravity.

Phase IV: The Power Position

See Section 10.4

While the balance position is the most important phase, the power position is the phase where the most flaws are likely to occur. The power position involves using the legs and hips to create velocity. Take a look at many major league pitchers today. They have tree trunks for legs. Yet to use the legs properly requires a series of things to happen—and when one or two don't happen, the pitch and pitcher are affected.

From the balance position, the raised leg should land in line with home plate. Many players lunge or jump toward home in the power position. Pitchers should be taught to avoid lunging. The pitcher's lead foot should land in a spot very similar to where the lead foot lands in the batting stride. When the lead foot lands, the back foot drives toward home and the hips explode, which produces power. Placing a pitcher in the power position, and having her throw to home is a good teaching strategy. When the ball leaves the pitcher's hand, the front foot should have the toe pointed toward home plate.

As the lead foot lands, the hands have already separated and the glove hand points toward home plate. The throwing hand extends down across the thigh, and then moves to a shoulder-high position behind the player (refer to the "thigh, high five" position in Chapter 3). Allowing the ball to pass next to the ear and not across the thigh will inflict stress on the elbow. This mechanical flaw should be corrected regardless of a pitcher's success. Trading success for a player's health should never be contemplated.

As the throwing arm comes forward to deliver the ball to home, the arm should be in an "L" position when it passes the head. The glove arm should now be tucked into the body to produce more torque and whip in the throwing motion. These two motions should be done simultaneously.

When the arm is in the "L" position, the player's weight should not shift completely to the front leg. Many players shift their weight too quickly onto the front foot, which results in losing power from the legs. As the arm is going forward toward home, the back leg and hips should be generating power to propel the ball faster to the catcher. In essence, the muscles of the legs and torso are helping to accelerate the arm.

In releasing the ball, the player should let go of the ball in front of the body. An incorrect release point, too early or late, will produce a ball thrown too high or low in the strike zone. When the ball is released, the hand should be pointed toward home, as though the pitcher was pointing at the catcher.

 *See Section 10.5*

Phase V: The Follow-through

In regard to technique, following-through is the least mechanically complex of the five phases of pitching. The follow-through has one specific purpose. It continues the throwing motion, even after the ball has left the pitcher's hand. After the ball's released, the throwing arm (of a right-handed pitcher) should continue its downward descent and finish on the outside of the left knee. The throwing hand should almost sweep the dirt. Some players stop the throwing motion after releasing the ball, which creates less velocity and can lead to injury.

After the ball is released, and the hand continues its downward descent, the leg pushing off the pitching rubber should swing around. The player should then be in a good fielding position. If the pitch is hit, the pitcher needs to become the fifth infielder. The follow-through, done correctly, should lead to a balanced stance, with the pitcher facing home plate.

Off-speed Pitches   Earlier in the chapter, it was mentioned that the best pitch a player can throw is a strike. However, strikes can be thrown fast or slow. When facing a good team, a pitcher needs to have more than a fastball. While there are many types of pitches to choose from, a young arm is physically able to handle only a few.

Curve balls

The curve ball should not be thrown by a player under the age of fourteen years old. No exceptions. The arm is not mature enough until approximately this age to handle the strain of throwing the curve. Players on opposing teams may do it, and the pressure to throw a curve ball at a young age is incredible. Coaches should resist the pressure and tell players to refrain from throwing the curve ball until the muscles and ligaments are mature enough to handle this pitch. Players who throw curve balls at a young age have a high risk of developing arm problems. In any case, there are equally effective pitches that do not injure the arm.

Change-up

The best pitch a young pitcher can learn to throw is the change-up. The throwing motion for this pitch does not place added stress on the arm, and the main difference from the fastball is the grip.

The change-up has the same effect on a hitter as a curve -ball. The reason for throwing the curve is to force the hitter to shift too soon to his front foot and swing weakly. The change-up, when thrown correctly, does the same exact thing. As a matter of fact, the change-up is even more effective than the curve for two reasons.

First, the change-up does not spin and looks the same coming out of the pitcher's hand as the fastball. In contrast, the curve ball requires the pitcher to snap the wrist and produce a spinning motion with the ball. A good hitter can spot the wrist action and wait for the pitch to curve. With a change-up, the batter will be fooled because the motion is identical to the fastball.

The second reason the change-up is more effective than the curve ball is its rarity. How many hitters see a good change-up in youth leagues? If a young player has a second pitch, it is usually a curve ball. Disguise and surprise are ingredients that make the change-up more effective than the curve.

Eric Gagne, one of the better closers in Major League Baseball, has two dominant pitches: fastball and change-up. Even though major league hitters know this fact, they still can't hit Gagne's pitches. He is not alone when it comes to major league pitchers who have effective change-ups. If a poll were taken among major league hitters, the change-up would rank among the toughest—if not the toughest—pitches to hit.

 *See Section 10.6*

How to Throw the Change-up

Many young pitchers think they know how to throw the change-up, but few execute this pitch correctly. Slowing down the arm and floating the ball toward home is not an effective way to throw a change-up.

For a change-up, the ball is gripped with two seams. Take the throwing hand, put it in front of you, and spread the fingers out as though you are giving someone a high-five. Place the two middle fingers on the two seams running parallel to one another. The other two fingers should extend on either side of the ball. The thumb should be placed directly underneath the ball. The ball should be placed deeper in the hand, but still only in the fingers. Resistance from the deep grip reduces the speed of the pitch. Throw the ball like a fastball.

Many pitchers want to throw the "circle change." The problem with throwing the circle change at a young age is the size of a young pitcher's fingers. The circle change is a pitch that is a little different from the straight change-up. The thumb and index finger slide closer together so the tips of the fingers touch. The fingers touching one another produce an "O" shape (hence the "circle"). When the ball is thrown, the wrist turns away, and the two fingers producing the "O" push the ball away. This makes the ball not only lose speed, but produces a dropping effect in that same direction. Because a young pitcher's fingers are small, the "O" cannot be fully formed and accuracy is lost. A pitcher should not throw the circle change until the fingers are long enough and the straight change-up is mastered. More times than not, the straight change-up will have movement because of the two-seam grip, and will tumble downward when thrown.

The change-up moves about ten miles per hour less depending on the velocity, when thrown effectively. This slight change of speed is enough to fool the hitter and disguises the pitch.

Drills Numerous drills can improve a pitcher's mechanics. When performing pitching drills, it is important to limit the number of pitches and to monitor progress. Having a player throw too much will have detrimental effects on the rotator cuff and a young arm.

Chapter 11 focuses on correcting pitching flaws, and presents a variety of drills. Here are a few of the more effective drills to use with pitchers.

Progression Drills

 *See Section 10.7*

Pitchers need a partner for this drill, or a catcher. With the players spread approximately twenty feet apart, one player serves as a catcher while the other pitches. The pitcher works on the fundamentals while throwing to a person in the catching position. The shortened distance allows for the player to throw with less velocity, and the focus of the drill is to use good mechanics and improve control. *Note:* all skills mentioned in this chapter, from the balanced position to the follow-through, can be taught and reinforced without having to throw hard. The pitcher does not need to throw from a mound when working on the fundamentals. The progression drill is great for working with more than one pitcher and allows for the coach to instruct a player more effectively.

Low-High-Low-Throw Drill

See Section 10.8

The low-high-low-throw drill can be done while working on the progression drills. With a player in the catching position approximately twenty feet way, the pitcher can use this drill to work on balance. For this drill, the wind-up is eliminated. The pitcher stands with the lead shoulder pointing toward the catcher. The stance resembles the stretch position, but with both feet together. The coach gives the command, "Low." The player then lifts the lead leg approximately six inches off the ground and holds it. The second command, "High," and the player lifts the leg and gets into the balance position, as explained in the "Balance Position" section. The next command, "Low," and the player returns the leg back to the original position (approximately six inches off the ground). The player throws the ball to the catcher when the final command is given, "Throw." The pitcher needs to demonstrate complete control and balance throughout the drill. The eyes should be focused on the catcher throughout the drill.

Power Position Drill

See Section 10.9

Partners should be about 25 feet apart for the power position drill. The drill teaches pitchers to use their legs while throwing. The players should already have their legs spread apart. The position is similar to that of a pitcher who's already taken his or her stride from the mound. Players may get too extended and not use their legs when pitching. Stand beside a player and mark where the glove-side foot lands. After marking it, have him or her put their foot in the mark and throw the ball from that spot using their legs. Finding out how little (or much) the legs are used is important in the learning process.

Make sure the legs are spread apart in a good, balanced position. The distance is similar to a three-point stance in football, or a batter's position after already taking a stride. The "scope" is already lined up and the thrower is standing in a position comparable to a pitcher's position in the stretch. With both hands out in front of the player, the thrower should load up on the back-side. When "back-side" is mentioned, the term refers to rocking back on the back leg, similar to what a boxer does who's about to deliver a powerful punch. It is important that the head does not go past the back leg. Such a position is referred to as "overloading." Using the legs allows the pitcher to throw harder and reduces arm stress.

Spot the Dot Drill

Position a catcher approximately twenty-five feet from the pitcher. The distance is lessened to prevent over-exertion (the drill can be done from the pitching mound). The catcher should have on the catching equipment. Four different colors of tape should be placed on the catcher: one on each knee, and one on each shoulder. The catcher should have four different colors on four different spots (numbers can be used too). Before the pitcher throws, the catcher or coach should call out a color for the pitcher to hit. The pitcher needs to use good mechanics and work on hitting the target. The drill is great for learning to locate pitches and develop control.

Summary Pitching is an art. The great pitchers, from Roger Clemens to Mariano Rivera, will confess the secrets to pitching are proper mechanics and conditioning. There is no magical tool or training device for turning a pitcher into a flame-thrower. The secret to becoming a great pitcher lies in simplicity. To become a good pitcher, a player needs to look no further than the basic fundamentals. Remember to keep it simple, and the best way to practice is by throwing—carefully and correctly.

Nine Pitching Flaws and How to Fix Them

PITCHERS should be treated like patients in the emergency room. Attention to their problems must be immediate. A pitcher with problems in the delivery is not only a potential detriment to the team but also may be harming him or herself. Just as hitters have drills to correct flaws, so do pitchers.

While the following flaws and subsequent drills are the most common, the K.I.S.S. (**K**eep **I**t **S**imple, **S**on) method will again be used. This means the drills are kept as simple as the basic mechanics of pitching itself.

1. The Ball is Coming Out of the Hand with Poor Rotation—Earth Ball

When a pitcher is throwing a fastball, the ball needs to have backward rotation after leaving the hand. The backward rotation indicates that the player is throwing the ball over the top and not turning the wrist upon release. To obtain maximum velocity and ensure safety, the ball needs to rotate backwards off of the two fingers on top of the ball. The thumb serves as a rest for the two fingers to snap downward.

When done incorrectly, the ball will spin sideways. This spinning motion resembles the sideways rotation of the Earth. An "Earth ball" is thrown when a player incorrectly snaps the wrist or releases the ball at an awkward arm angle. The elbow absorbs a lot of stress when the ball spins sideways. The flaw needs to be fixed to increase accuracy and reduce the risk of an elbow injury.

Pitching Flaws

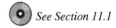 *See Section 11.1*

 This symbol indicates reference to Companion DVD for video instruction

A great drill for correcting the "Earth ball" involves two players, or one player and a wall. The two players need to stand approximately five feet apart. The player with the ball should be wearing a glove. With the throwing elbow in the glove out in front of the body, the player needs to line up the glove with his or her partner. While not moving the throwing arm or glove, the player isolates the wrist for this drill. The player takes the ball back, then forward, producing a wrist snap with backward ball rotation. The ball should be gripped with four seams and held properly (see Chapter 3). The player receiving the ball should give a target with the glove. The key is not to worry about velocity, but concentrate on developing backward rotation and a proper grip.

To help players see the proper rotation, the ball can be marked with a colored line 360 degrees around the baseball. With the line between the two fingers on top of the ball, the backward rotation will allow the line to be seen when the ball is thrown. If the ball doesn't have backward rotation, the line will not be visible.

As the player gets better at this drill, the forearm can be moved backward, then forward, to build on the wrist snap. The colored ball can be used for all throwing drills to allow for visual feedback. Use a magic marker or paint to draw the line on the ball.

 *See Section 11.2*

2. The Pitcher is Falling to the Left or Right of the Pitching Mound

When a pitcher strides toward home plate, the lead foot should land directly in line with the catcher. If a player is falling to the right or left of home plate after delivering the ball, check the lead foot. Pitchers have a tendency to stride to the right or left of home plate. To throw the ball consistently, a direct approach needs to be taken with the lead foot. Not only does the falling flaw affect accuracy, but the power generated by the hips and legs is minimized. The arm has to overcompensate for the lack of torso power, and injury is possible.

The next time a pitcher commits this flaw, draw a line in the dirt from the pitcher towards home plate. The line doesn't need to be long. It only needs to be drawn in the area of the landing stride foot. The pitcher should be told to go through the pitching motion and throw balls to home plate. The pitcher should be instructed to place the stride foot on the line. Landing to the right or left of the line indicates a mechanical flaw.

3. Dropping the Throwing Elbow

See Section 11.3

Since the pitching mound is elevated, the pitcher throws the ball at a downward angle. Perhaps tempted by this slight grade plus gravity, many pitchers drop the throwing elbow as the arm goes forward to deliver the ball. When you put the two facts together, throwing from an elevated position and dropping the throwing elbow, the physics do not add up. On the one hand, the ball needs to be thrown on a downward trajectory. On the other, dropping the throwing elbow elevates the ball. The pitcher needs to get the elbow up, so the ball starts high. At the same time, the downward force of the hand and forearm will in turn produce the ideal ball path.

The pitching elbow should be approximately shoulder high when the arm gets into the "L" position as it passes the head. This position is ideal for trajectory, maximum velocity, and safety.

A drill for pitchers who drop the back elbow requires, of all things, a batting tee. With the pitcher down on the throwing-side knee, place a tee under the throwing arm at the "L" position along side of the throwing-side hip. The tee needs to be as high as the player's armpit. Have the player throw from this position to a target. If the player drops the elbow, the tee will be hit. The elbow will clear the tee if the player throws with the correct mechanics. Make sure to keep the tee close to the player's body, so the arm has to go over the tee.

4. Unbalanced Player

See Section 11.4

Balance is the key to pitching. Pitchers who lose their balance lose velocity, control, and possibly their rotator cuff. Throwing from a balanced position allows the pitcher to set up correctly and control the body. The windup is where many players begin to be off balance. More movement equals more problems.

The idea is not to cookie-cut every player into the same type of pitcher. Pitchers should be allowed to develop a sense of style and personal flair. The game of baseball would lose its diversity and wouldn't be as interesting if the Fernando Valenzuelas and Orlando Hernandez's (El Duque) of the world didn't exist. These professional pitchers, whose windups are unique, still maintain a balanced position before throwing. Balance should never be sacrificed, and neither should a unique style, *once* the proper balance has been obtained.

Here is a drill to teach balance. Have the player lift the leg that rises during the pitching motion. When the player has the leg raised to its highest height (parallel to the ground), have the player hold the leg in the position for a five-count. The player should be looking toward home and be totally balanced. Swaying back and forth or not standing still means the player needs to change some things. One great tip is to bring the glove and throwing hand together, and rest them on the lifted leg. Since the center of gravity is in the belt region, the hands help keep the body centered. Lifting them too high over the head or bringing them too low will make the pitcher lose balance. After the five-count, the player should throw to the target. Doing this repeatedly will teach the player to stay balanced.

Another good drill is the "low-high-low-throw" drill, described in chapter 10. A friend of mine, a minor league pitcher, demonstrated this drill at my camp last summer. The pitcher starts from the stretch position. This is the position pitchers are in when runners are on base and can take a lead. While in the stretch position, the coach yells out, "Low." The player lifts the lead foot off the ground about six inches. The second command, "High," tells the player to lift the leg until it is parallel to the ground. The third command, "Low," has the player lower the leg to the first position again about six inches off of the ground. The last command, "Throw," tells the player to throw to the target. This drill is great for teaching balance throughout the entire throwing sequence. Again, the object is not to throw hard, but rather to throw with good balance.

 *See Section 11.5*

5. Arm Slot Problems/Control Issues

A pitcher can do everything correctly, from the wind-up to the balance position, but still have control issues. One big reason may be due to incorrect arm slots. An "arm slot" refers to the location of the arm when the ball is released to home. Releasing the ball too soon (ball sails high) or too late (ball goes low) in the throwing motion leads to erratic pitches. Pitchers need to learn the various arm slots and how to adjust them when trying to throw a high or low strike. Throwing the ball down the middle every time at the same height is a recipe for giving up a lot of runs. A pitcher can learn to use various arm slots to his or her advantage, and also make adjustments if the ball is unintentionally going high or low.

Here is a fun game that teaches the different arm slots. With a target placed at home plate (using a pitching net or other device), draw lines (or use ribbons or rope) every ten feet between the pitching mound and second base (approximately three lines). With a bucket of balls nearby, have the pitcher start on the regulation mound. Using good mechanics, the pitcher should throw balls until the target is hit. Once the target is hit once, the player should move back to the next line. The pitcher uses good pitching mechanics again, and when the target is hit the player can move back to the next line. This continues until the pitcher finishes at the back line. The distances and number of throws should be limited based on the player's age and arm sensitivity.

A game can be played by seeing who can hit the target using the fewest number of throws. The drill teaches the player to make adjustments with the arm slots, or where the ball is released. The game can be reversed, with the player starting at the back line and moving forward. Either way, the game and number of pitches should be monitored to prevent pitchers from exceeding their limit.

6. Trouble Spotting the Ball/Hitting the Desired Location

See Section 11.6

Being able to locate the ball is an art. Pitchers need to learn to throw the ball to the desired spot in the strike zone. Pitchers who can do this have a distinct advantage on the batter. Once the correct mechanics are learned, practicing locating the ball is important for developing accuracy.

Place a catcher approximately twenty-five feet from the pitcher. The distance is reduced to prevent over-exertion (the drill can be done from the pitching mound). The catcher should be wearing catching equipment. With four different colors of tape, place one color on each knee, and one on each shoulder. The catcher should have four different colors on four different spots (numbers can be used too). Before the pitcher throws, the catcher or coach should call out a color for the pitcher to hit. The pitcher needs to use good mechanics and work on hitting the target.

See Section 11.7

7. Over-rotation or Arm Wrap

When a pitcher leaves the balance position, the delivery should be direct and explosive toward home plate. In some instances, a player will over-rotate with the upper body, and the arm wraps behind the head. The "scope," or lead shoulder, becomes misaligned with home plate, and the chest faces the shortstop. This over-rotation makes it difficult for the

Figure 11.1 *Fence drill to avoid arm wrap.*

pitcher to throw accurately to the catcher. Wrapping the arm around the head creates a flaw that could injure the arm and prevents the throwing motion from coming over the top.

Over-rotation can be corrected by placing the pitcher's back near a wall or fence and having the pitcher throw to a catcher. The back should be almost touching the wall for this drill. The reason for the wall is to prevent arm wrap. If the player over-rotates, the hand will hit the wall when the pitcher delivers it to the catcher. The wall will be untouched if the correct throwing motion is used.

See Section 11.8

8. Not Using the Legs

The legs provide the power for a pitcher. Using the legs is essential for obtaining maximum velocity. Not only do the legs provide power, but they ease the amount of stress placed on the arm. Learning to use the legs at an early age will reduce the risk of injury.

A good drill for teaching players to use the legs is the no-stride drill. The pitcher will get into the power position from the start. This position is similar to that of a pitcher who's already taken his or her stride from the mound. Stand beside a player and mark where the glove-side foot lands. After marking it, have him or her put their foot on the mark and throw the ball from that spot using the legs. Finding out how little (or much) the legs are used is important in the learning process. Make sure the legs are spread apart in a good, balanced position. The distance is similar to a three-point stance in football, or a batter's position after already taking a stride. The "scope" is already lined up, and the thrower is standing in a position comparable to a pitcher's position in the stretch. With both hands out in front of the player, the pitcher should load up on the back-side. Again, the position is similar to that of a boxer ready to throw a punch. Also, avoid overloading, i.e., bringing the head back past the back leg. The pitcher drives with the back leg, explodes with the hips, and throws the ball to the catcher. No stride should be taken, and the feet do not need to move for this drill. Learning to use the legs is the focus.

9. Over-striding

See Section 11.9

When a pitcher strides toward home, he or she can over-stride, a flaw that reduces power. "Over-striding" is when a player steps too far with the lead foot toward home. The player becomes sprawled out, or has the legs in an uncomfortable position. The lead foot needs to land sooner in order to get optimal hip explosion and drive with the back leg. Pitchers who have this flaw usually get out on the front side too early, and the back foot drags off the mound without force.

To correct this flaw, a block of wood or brick is needed. Find the optimal spot for the landing of the pitcher's lead foot. Make a line in the dirt just past the stride foot's optimum position. If the player over-strides, the line will be touched or crossed. This is the first part of the drill.

The second part of the drill uses the block. Place the block in front of the pivot foot, which is the foot against the pitching rubber. When the player throws home, the back foot should lift and clear the block. If the player is over-striding, the back foot will drag and hit the block.

The combination of the line in front of the stride foot, and the block in front of the pivot foot will assist pitchers in getting into a good power position.

Summary

Keeping a pitcher's arm healthy should be the #1 concern for players, parents, and coaches. Correct mechanics are the way to a healthy arm. Flaws are eliminated when correct mechanics are used, and this chapter has provided drills for practicing the right pitching techniques. The longer a pitching flaw is left unchanged, the greater the risk of a young player injuring the arm.

Remember to always use the K.I.S.S. method when dealing with pitching mechanics. Coaches and players typically look for a magic antidote, for instance, the latest training technique or the newest product on the market. The magic of pitching lies in the basics of the motion.

Lastly, don't let players throw curveballs at a young age. When the player is old enough (around the age of 14), a curve ball can be taught. There are many other ways to fool hitters that are less harmful to the arm.

The pitching decisions made as a coach, parent, and player are important. The next time a young pitcher is throwing a no-hitter, and it is the last inning for the league championship, will you have the integrity to take him out if the pitch count maximum has been reached? Or will you send the pitcher back out there to win the championship, and possibly hurt his or her arm?

CHAPTER 12

Base Running

THE object of the game of baseball is to score runs. Unless only home runs are hit, scoring involves running the bases. Navigating the bases correctly can be the difference between winning and losing close games. Like all other facets of the sport, base running involves specific skills that can improve a player's game.

Not everyone likes to run. Learning to run the bases can be tedious for young players. As a player, one thing I dreaded was the base running portion of practice. Its importance, however, cannot be overstated. The skills necessary for running the bases are covered in this chapter. For players to enjoy and learn the skills, coaches must make them fun. This chapter will show you how to make running the bases a welcome part of practice.

Base running begins even before a player sets foot on the base paths. The player on-deck in the batting circle plays an important role too. The player on-deck is responsible, once the batter makes contact, for removing any objects from around home plate (bat or helmet). A bat or helmet can become an obstacle and possibly injure a runner or the catcher at home plate. Tell the batter on-deck to remove these items as soon as the batter leaves the batter's box. In the case of a walk, the batter on-deck should be responsible for retrieving the bat and tossing it towards the dugout.

Another responsibility for the on-deck player is communication. If a runner is rounding third and attempting to come home,

On-Deck

 See Section 12.1

 *This symbol indicates reference to Companion DVD for video instruction*

the on-deck player (and only the on-deck player) needs to be positioned behind home plate to let the runner know whether to slide or stay standing. The player should not impede the catcher or umpire, but should be in full view of the runner. While yelling, the player may also use hand signals. Hands over the head signify to remain standing up; hands waving downward signals that the runner needs to slide. Waving the arms downward to the right or left indicates which direction the player should slide. Teach these hand signals as ways the on-deck batter can help the runner heading towards home plate.

The dugout plays a role too. If you are in a league that allows leading off the bases, the dugout can keep an eye on the pitcher and watch for pick-off moves. If the pitcher throws to first to try and pick off the runner, the players on the bench should yell "Back." Teaching the players to communicate and help baserunners keeps everyone involved and encourages teamwork.

Teaching Tip

Teaching a player where to stand to direct a runner rounding third and coming home is important. A player does not want to interfere with the catcher, umpire, or runner coming home. The player should be approximately ten feet behind home plate, but on the first base side of the playing field. If a line was drawn from third base to home, the player should be standing on that line if it were extended another ten feet. This way the runner can clearly see the signaling player.

Home to First

 *See Section 12.2*

Beating Out a Grounder

When a ground ball is hit, running quickly down the baseline is essential. One word describes a baserunner all coaches like to see: hustler. Running down the baseline on a ground ball should be done with 100% effort. The batter should be taught to expect a fielder to bobble or misplay the ball. Easing up and assuming an out will be made are not an option.

To get down the baseline quickly, the batter must get a good jump out of the batter's box. When contact is made, the player needs to leave the batter's box and run right away. Hesitation gives fielders more time to make a play. In fact, players who rush to first from the batter's box can force fielders to hurry, thus increasing the possibility of errors.

When running down the baseline, players should take a direct route toward first. The shortest distance between two points is a straight line. The batter should run to the right of the first base line and stay on the path the whole way to first base.

Once at first, the player should make contact with the front of the base. This part of the base is the side closest to the runner. Stepping in the middle or the back of the base can cause injury. Bases are slippery, and the back of the base puts the ankle in a precarious position. It doesn't matter which foot touches the base. The foot closer to the bag should be the one that first touches it.

Figure 12.1 *Looking to the right.*

Players should be instructed to run all the way *through* first base. Lunging at the base, or taking a huge leap, will only slow the runner. The batter should run to a spot approximately five feet past the bag.

After making contact with the base, the player must put on the brakes and slow down. The head should turn to the right. If the ball is overthrown, the runner can see it instantly. Too many times on an overthrow the player will not notice until people in the stands or in the dugout start hollering. This can be a delay of two or three seconds, the time needed to be safe at second. Hollering can be muffled and cause confusion. Looking to the right after touching the bag helps the runner make his or her own decision on whether or not to advance.

If a player's called safe at first, he or she should be taught to turn to the right when going back to the base. Turning to the left can be misunderstood as attempting to go to second. Many players have been tagged out for turning in the wrong direction when coming back to first base.

Lastly, instruct players not to slide into first base. Sliding is not faster than running through the bag. There is only one occasion where sliding is beneficial. If the first baseman jumps in the air or has to come off the base on a poor throw, sliding is effective. In this situation, the first baseman needs to make a tag on the runner, and avoiding the tag requires sliding.

 *See Section 12.3*

Base Hit to the Outfield, or Extra Bases

On a base hit to the outfield, the batter's footwork around the bases and down the baseline are different. The player still needs to get a good jump out of the batter's box, and hustling is a given.

The mindset for a player hitting the ball to the outfield, whether a line-drive or ground ball, should always be to get to second. The player needs to think "double" from the time the ball leaves the infield. This mindset encourages players to make a hard turn at first, and possibly advance to second on a ball bobbled by the outfielder.

Running down the first base line, the player needs to "banana out" about fifteen feet from first base. "Banana out" refers to running to the right in the shape of a banana towards a base. After first base is touched, the banana out route forms a straight line to second base. The "banana" should not be too curved. Running too much to the right will take the runner too far from first. The banana should be just enough to get the player on a path to second base.

After the "banana out" move, and as the runner is turning towards second, he needs to touch first base in the best way to keep moving. The base has four sides. The side facing second base should be hit with the right foot to drive toward second.

The runner should have a view of the ball and make a decision whether to run to second, or stay at first. In either case, the runner should make a hard turn at first base. Keep running at top speed until the outfielder cleanly fields the ball. If the ball is bobbled or misplayed, the runner continues running fast to second base. If the ball is fielded cleanly, the runner must slow down—but should still be ready to move on to second. Even on a base hit that an outfielder picks up smoothly, there is always the possibility of a bad or mishandled throw into the infield. Either situation is an opportunity to advance to second base.

Teaching Tip

Rounding first base properly should be drilled regularly at practice. The player should never give up on a ball to the outfield, and should always have the mindset that the ball will be misplayed by the outfielder. Being aggressive on the base paths puts pressure on the defense. Coaches can stand at first base and call out scenarios when players round first. For example, a player makes the turn at first base and the coach calls out, bobble. The player continues running and slides into second base. Silence from the coach might signify the outfielder cleanly fielded the ball. The coach can create his or her commands for the drill.

Stealing

Stealing bases is an art, and explaining the art can be complicated. Still, techniques exist for teaching players how to steal, and the ability to steal can be a valuable asset to a team. Every runner can become a successful base-stealer.

Before taking a lead, players should make sure the pitcher has the ball on the mound. A big lead off first base should be taken in order to draw a throw from the pitcher. Drawing a throw from the pitcher allows the runner, and the rest of the team, to see the type of pick-off move the pitcher possesses. Be sure to lean toward the base and anticipate a throw. If the pitcher does not throw to first, get a little bigger lead the next time. The whole purpose of this strategy is to see the pitcher's move.

The distance away from first base for a lead varies for every player. A general rule of thumb is to get a large enough lead so the player can take a

Figure 12.2 *Taking a lead.*

small step and dive to first. This can be taught during practice. Experiment with the size of the lead for different players. One length will not fit all.

When leading off, a runner should never take her eyes off of the pitcher. Receiving signs from the coach is done while the runner is still on the bag, before a lead is taken. A shuffling of the feet should occur when taking a lead. The shuffling is a simple side-to-side slide step. It should be done under control and not too fast. The feet do not cross. The shuffle allows a runner to dive back if the pitcher throws to first.

 See Section 12.4

While leading off first, the runner's focus is on one spot . . . the pitcher's feet. For a right- handed pitcher, there are only two things to watch. If the left foot picks up, the pitcher must go home. If the right foot picks up, the player must throw to first. Watching these two indicators provides a signal that can to allow for a quicker first step to second base. I call them "Green light-Red light." If the left foot picks up, green light. If the right foot picks up, red light. Focusing on these two indicators, instead of on the whole pitching motion, will make a better base stealer.

Teaching Tip

The pitcher's feet are indicators whether to steal or retreat to first base. Be careful the pitcher doesn't move both feet at the same time and spin when throwing the ball to first. The important foot is the back foot, or the foot on the pitching rubber. If that foot leaves the rubber, the pitcher must throw to first base. Green light, red light is effective when the main focus is on the red light (foot on the rubber). If the right foot doesn't move, but the left does, the runner should steal.

 See Section 12.5

With a left-handed pitcher, the task for the runner leading off first base becomes more difficult. The pitcher can now keep the runner in view. There is a fine line between a throw home and a throw to first base. Here is what the runner should do with a lefthander on the mound. First, take a slightly shorter lead. When the pitcher lifts the lead (right) leg, steal second. Go immediately. Stealing in this way is a gamble. On the other hand, it is hard to wait until the left-handed pitcher throws home to start to steal. Even if the runner successfully reads the difference between a pitcher's throw to the plate and move towards first, deciding which requires leaving a little later. Taking the shorter lead and leaving as soon as the pitcher lifts the right leg gives the runner a big jump. If the pitcher does throw to first, the first baseman must make a good catch and throw to second. A lot of runners still make it to second, even when they leave on a lefthander's leg movement. Although it is not a fine science and indeed is risky, it is effective and a high-percentage play when done at the right moment.

The first steps in stealing are the most important. Which foot do you step with first? The cross-over step is the quickest movement when stealing. Most players step with the right foot first. This is a wasted movement. It is small and ineffective. Take the first step with the left foot. The left foot should cross over the right. When the crossover occurs, the right arm should pull and tuck into the body and the left arm should pump forward. The center of gravity needs to stay low, with the body being bent over. The first step is often the difference between being safe or out at second base.

After the third step, take a quick glance in at home plate. This quick glance will let the runner see the outcome of the pitch. In the case of a batter making contact, it becomes even more important. A runner must freeze on a line drive or fly ball with fewer than two outs. If the ball is hit and caught, the runner needs to return to first as quickly as possible.

 *See Section 12.6*

If leads are not allowed in your league, the starting position should be like that of a sprinter. One foot should be on the base, and the other pointing toward second base. The knees should be bent and the weight shifting toward second when the ball crosses home plate. This position allows for a good jump on a steal or hit ball.

Secondary Leads/Reading Down-Angle

 *See Section 12.7*

In the event a runner is not stealing, a secondary lead needs to be taken during the pitch. In a "secondary lead" the runner takes two hopping shuffles toward the next base as the pitcher throws. The motion is a hopping sideways, without crossing the feet. Landing on the second hop should be timed with the pitch crossing home plate, so that the runner's momentum is towards the next base.

Secondary leads not only close the distance to the next base, but they also help with a player's movement toward the next base. Even if your league does not permit leading off a base, a secondary lead can be taken. After the ball crosses home, the player can hop twice off of the base. In either situation, a runner needs to be aware that the catcher might try a quick- release throw behind the runner.

Another secret to good base running is reading down-angle. "Reading down-angle" occurs when the runner observes the path of the thrown ball from the pitcher. If the angle is downward and the ball looks like it is going to hop in front of the catcher, the runner instantly steals second. Why? The odds are against the catcher making a good block or "pick" of the ball and then throwing accurately to second base. Often a pitch hitting in front of home plate is blocked by the catcher. Yet even if this happens, the runner who takes off before the ball hits the dirt has a good chance of reaching second. Reading down angle gives the runner an advantage. It can be taught in practice. Players can be placed on first (or other bases), as the coach pitches to a catcher at home. On a good pitch, the runner moves back to the base. On a poor pitch, that is, one with a down angle, the runner breaks toward the next base.

Sliding

See Section 12.8

See Section 12.9

The purpose of sliding is to avoid a tag. There are three types of slides: the pop-up slide, hook slide, and headfirst slide.

The pop-up slide is a feet-first slide. When the runner reaches the base, the runner "pops up" into a standing position. This slide usually occurs on a play that is not very close. The runner uses the pop-up slide to stop momentum and quickly get back on his feet.

The hook slide is a feet-first slide into a base to avoid a close tag from the fielder. The player slides and tries to hook the right or left foot on the inside or outside corner of the base. If the tag is attempted by the fielder on the inside portion of the bag, the hook slide is performed on the outside corner of the base.

Figure 12.3 *Hook slide.*

With a hook slide, the body is farther away from the bag and the leg is extended laterally to reach the base. The body is kept away from the base, so the target is small and the tag difficult to make.

In a headfirst slide, the runner dives headfirst into he base. This type of slide is not recommended for youth players. The chances of injury are increased, especially on the hands or head, either by being hit with a ball or cut by spikes.

 *See Section 12.10*

Teaching Tip

If the headfirst slide is permitted, both hands of the runner should be holding a batting glove. Holding a batting glove in each hand keeps the fingers from being exposed. The hand needs to grip the glove with a fist. While this is not going to eliminate possible injury, it does reduce the risk of the fingers getting hurt.

When a runner attempts to slide into a base, the slide needs to start approximately six to eight feet in front of the base (the distance varies for each player). Sliding too late, when the runner is very close to the base, will jam the legs and body into the base in an awkward manner. Players should be taught to start the slide in ample time to reduce the risk of injury.

When sliding feet first, do not slide on the buttocks. The correct way to slide is on the right outer-thigh (and right buttock). Sliding on the right buttock turns the front of the body away from a thrown ball and helps avoid injury. On a throw from the outfield, the left outer-thigh should be used to slide. Turning away from the throw protects the vital parts of the body.

Teaching Tip

The best time to practice sliding is on a rainy day. Kids love to play in the rain (adults too!). The next time practice is interrupted because of rain, get your players out in the outfield and work on sliding. The wet grass is perfect for this. Not only will your team approach sliding with enthusiasm, but the grass provides a better cushion compared to the dirt infield.

As the player slides, tilting the head back slightly allows the body to glide faster along the ground. The more the head stays upright, the greater the chance the legs will dig into the ground or the knees will hit first.

First to Third Base Running

 *See Section 12.11*

A player on first base must sometimes try to advance to third base on a hit. Again, the straightest distance between two points is a straight line. The player needs to take a direct route toward second base. As the player approaches second, a very slight banana out should be used. The runner needs to curve out just enough to be lined up with third when second is touched.

Second base has four sides. As she rounds second, the runner's foot should push off the side facing third. This propels the player toward third. While either foot could be used, the right foot is optimal for a good push.

As second base is touched, the runner should look at the third base coach. There are four basic commands the coach can give the runner. The coach can tell the player to go home, stand up and hold at third base, slide into third because there is going to be a throw to the base, or stay at second base. The runner does not rely only on the third base coach to determine which of these to do. Relying solely on the third base coach to make a decision is not recommended. If the ball is hit to left field, a player can see the ball and make a decision as the play unfolds. When the ball is behind the runner, for example on hits to right field, the runner must depend exclusively on the third base coach for guidance.

Rounding Third

 *See Section 12.12*

The player moving towards third base needs to take a direct approach and also banana out to line up with home plate. As you are rounding third base, push off of the side of the base facing home plate. The runner should look at the third base coach when rounding the base. The coach will give a command of stay or go. In either case, obeying the coach is non-negotiable. The coach has a better view of the play than the runner, and his judgment dictates whether the player runs home or remains on third.

Be sure not to banana out too far when approaching third. The banana should be small enough to line up the player with home plate.

While learning about base running may not be as exciting as learning other baseball techniques, many games can be used to reinforce base running skills. Here are three.

4-3-2-1

See Section 12.13

Traditional wind-sprints or conditioning exercises are not necessary at baseball practice. Running the bases is a logical alternative, which has the extra advantage of helping youth players get into shape. One great drill to do at the end of practice is a 4-3-2-1. With the players standing in a line at home plate, each player takes a turn being a batter at home plate. The player simulates getting a base hit, and runs out a single. When the player gets halfway to first, the next player continues with the same activity. The drill continues until everyone has finished running out a single. After running through the base, the players should slowly jog to the back of the line. The drill requires the players to complete four singles, three doubles, two triples, and one home run.

A variation of this activity can be done. A 1-1-1-1 can be substituted for the 4-3-2-1. This would involve one single, double, triple, and home run. The number of singles, doubles, triples, and home runs can be determined by the coach and should be age-appropriate. The bases should be run properly, and the skills reinforced.

"Catch the Rabbit"

Eight players are needed to play this game. One player stands on each base (including home plate) on the infield (4 total players). The other four players stand at the midway point between a base. On the coach's signal, the players start to run around the bases. The object of the game is to tag the person in front of you. Once tagged, a player is out of the game and sits down on the side. The last person standing is declared the winner. The first four people tagged do not get a break. They run in the next game too.

Catch the Rabbit not only requires good base running technique, but is a great activity for building character. The last player standing is usually the one with the most fortitude on the team. Giving up is not in this player's vocabulary. When positioning players at their starting positions, be mindful of the match-ups. Placing a slower runner in front of a faster one is not recommended. The slower runner will be caught quickly and get discouraged. Try to position the players according to ability level.

Situational Running

Situational base running can be implemented during batting practice. Too often, batting practice involves one person hitting, and a lot of people standing around (see Chapter 13 on practice management for more on batting practice). Batting practice is a time where *all* players should be engaged in an activity. Base running is one of those activities. While a hitter is taking batting practice, runners can work on the secondary lead, or on running from first to third base. Good practice management allows all aspects of base running to be worked on during batting practice.

Summary While there are numerous situations and scenarios, the physical skills needed to run the bases are simple to teach and learn. Once these skills are learned, a strong foundation is built, to incorporate more advanced learning.

Running the bases isn't just about how fast a player can run. It is about angles, instincts, and hustle. Learning the fundamentals and applying them will help the team score more runs—and will help win ball games.

CHAPTER 13

Practice Management

ORGANIZING a practice is a coaching skill that encompasses all others. Fully engaging players on a regular basis requires planning, an arsenal of drills, and a knack for understanding where players can be improved. While running a practice is fairly straightforward, the successful coach has an orchestrated plan of attack.

Managing a well-organized practice is beneficial for the coach and players. The time saved, and then put to good use, is invaluable to the players' progress.

Managing a practice begins before the first pitch or crack of the bat. When the roster is given out and you know the players, sending a letter introducing yourself is a nice touch. Many players, when they find out who their coach is, are apprehensive. The letter should be typed at the right reading level and contain items such as the following:

Before the First Practice

- warm optimistic greeting
- expectations for practices and games
- schedule for the year (practice and games)
- contact information

With the letter, a flier can be included for the parents. The flier should specify a date and time for a parent meeting. The meeting is a great opportunity for parents to sign up as volunteers. This meeting is also your chance to answer questions, convey your philosophy on coaching, and make known rules and expectations. Getting all of this information into the right hands before the first practice can allow the first practice to be . . . a practice. It is also a welcoming gesture, and demonstrates you care and are accessible to the parents.

The final requirement's a game plan. The first practice should be well-scripted, with subsequent practices sketched out for the following week. The game plan will depend on the level coached. Seven- and eight-year-olds may need more drills for throwing properly and accurately, where twelve-year-olds should focus more on game situations. Understanding the level you coach and applying an age-appropriate game plan are important to be effective.

Teaching Tip

When making an outline for practice, be sure to build in backup plans. Things don't always go as planned when dealing with young kids. Sometimes things arise that require a change of plan from your scripted workout. Be flexible and have secondary drills or activities in case of an unexpected twist in the schedule.

First Practice   One year, I asked a boy how his first practice went. This kid loved baseball! What he proceeded to tell me was not only astonishing, but is a big reason why I continue to educate coaches at clinics. What was his response? He said, "We really didn't do much." I replied by saying, "Not much. What do you mean? You had practice last night. What did you do?" He said that he couldn't really figure it out, but they were timed from home to first, first to second, second to third, and third to home (four separate timing sessions). I asked him if that was it. He replied, "No. Then the coach dumped all of the balls all over the outfield and we ran around and picked them up." I was baffled. I asked him why they did that activity. He had no idea. He described this first practice with about ten percent of the enthusiasm he probably had on the day of the practice. It was like watching a kid on Christmas who found only clothes beneath the tree.

The first practice is the most important. The players show up full of hope and anticipation. The parents usually hang around to soak in the sights and sounds. The next couple hours will have a lasting impression on each and every player. Without a doubt, the first practice needs to be the best one of the year . . . and the most meaningful.

Make sure to start the first practice on time. If the first practice is supposed to start at 6 P.M., then 6 P.M. is when the players should be assembled and the practice begins. When players start arriving at 6:05, parents will get the picture that practice is not going to start on time. Many coaches wait for the stragglers to roll in to start practice. If parents drop the players off at 6:05, and practice has still not started, it sends the message that practice will not start until everyone arrives. Dropping players off late then becomes a chronic problem.

During the first practice, the coach needs to establish a routine. Each portion of practice needs to be devoted to a specific purpose or skill. Within each portion, expectations need to be established and the purpose of the time spent should be stressed. At the beginning, set a tone for how practice is going to be run the entire season.

During the first practice, split the players into groups. For the sake of explanation, let's say twelve players are on a team. Separate the players into four groups, one, two, three, and four. These groups will not change for the whole season. Players will always know what group they are in, and grouping will never take up any more time. These groups can be used for batting practice, breakout sessions, or even to get pictures taken. How many times on a field have you heard the phrase "Who hasn't hit yet?" Now, with predetermined groups, the number can be called and the players can hit according to group number. Once the last numbered group hits, all players have had a turn at the plate.

First 25 Minutes of Practice

Let me describe the first twenty-five minutes of an average practice. The players are dropped off at the field, anywhere from thirty minutes early to fifteen minutes late. The players put gear in the dugout, grab a ball, and start throwing. As other players arrive, the players follow the same pre-practice ritual until every player arrives. After approximately twenty minutes, the players are assembled and practice begins.

The first twenty-five minutes need to be a structured routine, since routines save time. Without routines, up to one quarter of the whole practice can be wasted on repeatable organizational tasks.

When players arrive, their gear should be placed in the dugout, and they should take a lap around the field. The jog around the field warms up the muscles for the stretching that occurs next. On his own, each player should go through a stretching routine that is modeled during the first practice. The player should stretch the entire body, with the arm stretches done to loosen the arm (see Chapter 2 for proper arm stretches). No player should touch a ball until the arm stretches are completed. The stretches will not only loosen the arm, but will also strengthen it. With the alarming number of arm injuries occurring in baseball, stretching and strengthening the arm must be a mandatory part of practice.

Once the stretches are completed, the player can now work on throwing accurately. The purpose of playing catch is not to loosen the arm. The arm stretching exercises have already accomplished this. With good mechanics already used, playing catch is an activity to work on throwing with accuracy. Players should be taught from the outset why throwing properly is important.

After the players have thrown for ten minutes, the coach needs to gather the players and give an overview of the practice schedule. Revealing the schedule will help put to rest the perennial, "What are we going to do now, coach?" A youth league coach in our area did something I really liked at the beginning of every practice. He asked a trivia question from a little baseball book he had. Not only was this a nice way to teach the history of the game, but the players seemed to enjoy trying to answer the question.

Batting Practice The most mismanaged part of practice is batting practice. Coaches give a player approximately six swings, while the rest of the team congregates on the field and talks. This type of batting practice occurs at all levels of play, from youth league to college ball. All players, not just the batter, need to be learning during batting practice.

Players have already been divided into groups (see section on "First Practice" in this chapter). Three or four players should be in each group (three is optimal). Group one will go in to hit first (vary the order for each practice). If twelve players are on a team, nine players remain. Each player should then play a position on the field. The coach usually pitches, so the ninth man can be the bagman. The bagman gathers the balls hit by the batter. The ball, when fielded by the players, should be thrown to the bagman who is stationed behind second base in shallow center field. If your youth league is fortunate to have a protective net, the bagman can stand behind the net for safety reasons. The bagman will help eliminate precious time during practice. When the coach runs out of balls to throw, the bagman is called in to replenish the balls. Many times players will retrieve a ball hit by the batter and toss it toward the pitching mound. When the coach needs more baseballs, the field looks like an Easter egg hunt. Picking up balls takes up at least fifteen minutes of valuable time during practice. The catcher should also have a bucket or bag to collect balls.

With everyone playing a position, many options are available for practicing defense. Each player can work on: footwork, reading the ball off of the bat, and situational scenarios. Defensive players can practice turning the double play, hitting the cut-off man, or simply getting the routine out. The scenarios are endless, and the coach can use discretion based on the needs of the team.

Instead of simply having each player take six swings, give players a purpose when conducting batting practice. Each and every swing should have a purpose. With three players in a group, one is hitting, the second is on deck, and the third is the go-pher. The "go-pher" is a player who collects balls hit foul during practice. This allows for the players on the field to assume their positions and not waste valuable time. Instead of hitting once and taking six swings, the players should hit in a series of rounds. Players should get three or four rounds when hitting, and the players should rotate after each round. The rotation is: go-pher to on-deck, on-deck to batter, then batter to go-pher.

One round should consist of four or five full swings. The first round is always a bunting round. Players should bunt two balls down the third base line, two balls down the first base line, and then a drag bunt (or squeeze bunt). Each player bunts until all members of his or her group have taken a turn. With the players grouped, working on bunt defense is an option for the defense, and all of the balls will be in the same area where they are ready to be picked up. If a bunt defense is not being practiced, the third and first baseman should be told to move in and field the bunts.

The second round, and consecutive rounds thereafter, are conducted with a purpose. Each swing should have an understood goal. The second round might have the objective of hitting the ball to the right side of the field. In the third round, players should be told to hit only grounders. The fourth round may be fly balls to the outfield to drive in a player from third with less than two outs. The scenarios are endless. One round can be chosen to allow the player to swing the bat freely. Working on situational hitting proves valuable once the games start, and situations develop where the ball must be put into play in a given way. Situational hitting also teaches bat control and lets each player know that he or she can—and often should—swing at a ball with an idea of where it should go.

Teaching Tip

Instead of throwing from the mound, move the "L" screen (if you are fortunate to have one) in to about twenty-five feet from home. Many coaches not only have trouble throwing strikes, but the coach's arm may not be as young as it used to be. This will help with control and saving the arm. It will also require the ball to be thrown slower because the hitter's reaction time is reduced.

Many players struggle to make contact during batting practice. It is not only embarrassing for the player, but the defense can fall asleep. A great variation of batting practice is soft toss batting practice. Incorporate the same grouping system and players at their defensive positions. The coach is positioned at home plate on the opposite side of the player. Instead of throwing from the mound, the coach tosses the ball for the player to hit. This is a great way to maximize the swings and it fosters success. The ball can be tossed for inside, outside, and down the middle strikes. Teaching the player how to drive the ball to all fields is a valuable tool. With soft toss batting practice, the player can learn to hit a ball more quickly than when it is thrown from the mound. It also allows the coach to be near the hitter. This allows for one-to-one instruction and also has the added benefit of being relatively private. While one coach is tossing batting practice, another can be on the field. After each pitch, the coach at the plate can instruct hitters, while the coach on the field can guide the fielders.

Batting practice is also a good time to work on situational base running. If more than twelve players are on a team, the extra players can be base runners. Again, all aspects of the game can be worked on, and the scenarios are endless. The players take more swings, the defense gets more practice, and the baserunners learn to navigate the bases. Remember: engage *all* kids in instruction 100% of the time.

One of the least stressed, yet most important, aspects of defense is the game or game-like situation. Youth baseball players need to understand situations and the differing responsibilities of playing each position. There are many ways to accomplish this task. From playing scrimmages to hitting balls in various scenarios with base runners, situations need to be practiced regularly.

Defense Management

A game that is fun and effective for teaching situations is the fungo game. Since the players are already split into groups, these form the teams for the game. With one player playing each position (including the pitcher position), each team takes a turn playing offense. The offensive team creates a batting order (which you should help create), and each player stands at the plate one at a time and throws the ball in the air and hits it. The object of the game is for the offense to score runs. The defense needs to get the offense out. If the player at the plate misses the ball, an out is charged to the team. If runners are left stranded on a base, and it is a player's turn to hit, an out is charged to the team too. Teams take turns playing offense, and the defensive players are substituted to fill vacant spots. Players should play various positions to learn the game. Fungo is great because it is competitive and intense. The players enjoy this game immensely. There's a lot of action, and the coaches can roam the field, pausing for teachable moments.

Another popular way to teach fundamentals is by hitting balls with a couple of players running the bases. The coach can manipulate the situation by hitting the ball to a desired location. Baserunners can be placed at bases to create situations that need practiced. When players are running from home to first during this activity, be sure to draw a line behind home plate for the runners to stay behind until the ball is struck. If players leave too early, the activity loses its effectiveness.

When working on situations, make sure the players communicate with one another. Communication is a skill that can be taught. The catcher is the quarterback on the baseball field, and he should take charge and yell out the number of outs after each batter. The rest of the players should echo the number of outs and alert each other to special situations, such as long leads by runners, areas where a batter tends to hit, or base coverage assignments.

If there was only one skill I had to choose for teaching defense, it would be moving the ball around the infield. Start the ball with the catcher, and let the players throw the ball from home to first, then from first to second, second to third, with the third baseman finishing the sequence by throwing home (the order can be reversed with the catcher throwing to third first and players moving the ball in the opposite direction.). This is called "throwing it around the horn." Most teams cannot make it around the horn more than once without an errant throw. Rehearsing this during each and every practice will pay dividends when it is game time.

While teaching situations is a high priority, the fundamentals of fielding need to be taught as well during practice (see chapters six through eight for positional fundamentals). Scheduling breakout sessions during practice is another way to work on position specific skills. Depending on the number of coaches on a team, breakout sessions can be split according to position. For example, if three coaches are available, the three stations can be infielders, outfielder, and pitchers. With pitchers being position players too in youth leagues, the pitching station may be one-on-one. The coach instructing the pitching station can remove pitchers one at a time to work on fundamentals or provide individualized instruction. The breakout sessions can vary from practice to practice.

Pitching Many coaches ask me how to teach pitching without hurting a player's arm at practice. Coaches make the mistake of not working their pitchers enough. Pitchers need to work on their mechanics more than any other player on the field. Poor mechanics and conditioning of the arm are the two main factors leading to injury. Mechanics can be worked on without throwing a ball. The main concerns for coaches should be: not to have a pitcher throw hard during the practice sessions, and limit the pitch count.

When splitting the team into groups during the first practice of the year, try to put all of the pitchers in one group. When breakout sessions are held, the group can work together on their pitching mechanics.

One way to hold a breakout session is to place all pitchers on the foul line in the outfield. Pitchers do not need to throw from the mound to work on their mechanics. Pair up the players in the group so one is a catcher, and the other a pitcher. The catcher should be approximately twenty feet away and in the catching position. The pitcher can go through mechanical drills and work on throwing strikes at a close distance (refer to Chapter 10 on pitching for drills). At such a close range, the pitcher cannot throw as hard, which alleviates stress on the player's arm. The focus during these drills should be on mechanics and control, not velocity.

During the preseason, or lulls within the season, pitchers need to pitch live to batters. This helps get the pitcher ready for games and gives hitters a chance to see pitches thrown at game speed. Make sure to limit the number of pitches when the pitchers throw to hitters. In the preseason the maximum number of "live" pitches should be twenty-five. At other times the number is limited by the game schedule and the frequency with which a player pitches.

Practice Time

The amount of time spent practicing varies according to age level. With six- to eight-year-old players, an hour is plenty of time. Keeping the attention span of a seven-year-old is not easy. Spending more than an hour can be tedious and boring for a young player. The time spent should be effective and fun. The purpose is to teach the fundamentals and instill a love for the game.

Conditioning vs. Base Running

Having players run wind-sprints or conditioning players at the end of practice has always baffled me. Instead of having players run sprints, incorporate base running to condition the players.

Chapter 12 emphasized the importance of base running in baseball and went over drills and skills to make players better at navigating the bases. There are many games and drills that can be performed at the end of a practice. Every practice should focus on one segment of base running, whether it is making the turn at first or tagging up at third base on fly balls to the outfield. Ending each practice with some sort of base running drill is a good routine to establish.

Practice Schedule Model

In schools, lesson plans are required from all teachers to script the goals and activities for the day and week. Coaches should learn to do practice plans. The plan does not need to be elaborate, or printed on a computer. The plan can be on scrap paper. If you have aspirations of being a complete coach, purchasing a three-ring binder is recommended, and the plans can be kept for filing purposes. All of the practices can be placed in the binder and consulted for future reference. This binder can also contain emergency information for all players, the schedule for the year, and any other pertinent information for the season. This organization will benefit the players and coaches. Below is a sample practice schedule for several days, assuming there are three coaches on the team. The breakout sessions will change each day for positions. For example, infielders may work on double plays on day 1, but on bunt defense on day 2:

DAY 1

6:00 – 6:25
   Players arrive and go through stretching, throwing for accuracy
6:25 – 6:45
   Breakout sessions (infielders, outfielders, pitchers)
6:45 – 7:30
   Batting practice
7:30 – 7:45
   Relays from the outfield to bases
7:45 – 8:00
   Base running (taking a secondary lead from first base)

DAY 2

6:00 – 6:25
   Players arrive and go through stretching, throwing for accuracy
6:25 – 6:45
   Breakout sessions (catchers, outfielders)
6:45 – 7:30
   Batting practice (soft toss batting practice . . . infield works double plays)
7:30 – 7:45
   Rundowns
7:45 – 8:00
   Base running (sliding)

DAY 3

6:00 – 6:25
   Players arrive and go through stretching, throwing for accuracy

6:25 – 6:45
    Breakout sessions (infielders, outfielders, pitchers)
6:45 – 7:30
    Batting practice
7:30 – 8:00
    Defensive situations

Summary

Managing a practice requires a coach to have organizational skills. Scripting a practice and following a plan minimize stress and maximize instructional time. While the plan is structured, a coach needs to be flexible too. There are days when the plan will fall apart due to uncontrollable circumstances. A coach needs to be able to adapt the plan and adjust accordingly. Teachable moments will also present themselves, and a new direction may need to be taken. Regardless of the situation, a plan benefits the players and makes a coach—and coaching time—more effective.

Practice Checklist

✓ All players have stretched their arms before throwing.
✓ Pitchers have worked on their mechanics.
✓ Batting practice had a purpose.
✓ Defensive situations and skills have been rehearsed.
✓ Base running has occurred.
✓ All players were engaged in activities 100% of practice time.
✓ All coaches were positive and enthusiastic.

age, of player
  and pitch count, 123
allergies,11
arc of ball
  for long-toss, 36
archery,
  and throwing hand, 27–28
arm bar, 50, 68
arm slots, 30
  in pitching, 138
arm wrap (flaw), 140
attitude
  for fielding, 81
  for hitting, 40

balance
  in hitting, 80
  in pitching, 137
banana out base running, 146, 152
base running, 143, 144
base stealing, 147, 148
  fielders' position and, 90
bat
  choosing size of, 51, 64
  extension during swing, 77
bat wrap (flaw), 50, 68
batter's box
  position in, 63
batting practice, 61, 158
  base running during, 154
Berkman, Lance, 60
body language
  coach's, 2
  positive, 2

Bonds, Barry, 52
boxing
  and hitting, 48, 52, 67–68, 71, 77, 79
  and pitching, 132, 141
  and throwing, 36
bunting, 57

Carroll, Will, 14
catch, playing
  teaching of, 27
catcher
  and onfield communication, 82
catching
  fly balls, 107
  ground balls, 82
change-up,
  how to throw, 129–130
character, 2, 4
Clemens, Roger, 132
communication
  on deck hitter and, 143
  on field, 82
  for fielders, 82
  on relay throws, 92
covering a base
  during steal attempt, 90
  curve ball, 129
  and young arm, 129
cutoff person, 111, 112
  for relay throws, 91

darts, 31
double-play, 95

elbows
  dropping during swing, 47
  in batting stance, 46–47
  in pitching, 137
  in throwing, 31
  stretches for, 17
emergency phone list, 11
encouragement, 7, 8
extension
  on swing, 78

fear of ball
  while batting, 64
feeding
  ball to double play pivot, 97, 100,
    101
feet, position of
  in base stealing, 149
  in catching, 119
  in fielding, 84–85
  in hitting, 43–44, 49
    open vs. closed, 49
fence, fielding ball near, 112–113
fielders
  position of, 81
  setting up, 82
finger pressure
  for throwing, 26
follow-through
  batting, 55
  pitching, 128
football
  three-point stance, 43, 65, 84, 132,
    141
force play, 100
four-seam grip, 24–26
  in fielding, 87
front arm bar, 50
fungo game, 161

Gagne, Eric, 129
Gibson, Mel, 28
Griffey, Ken, 55
grips
  for batting, 45, 65
  for bunting, 58–59
  four-seam, 24–25
  pitching, 124, 136
  pressure, 26
  two-seam, 25

ground balls
  double-play, 96–99
  fielding of, 82
  in outfield, 111
Gwynn, Tony, 64

hands
  position in fielding, 85–86, 88
  position on bat, 16
  position on bunts, 58
head
  position for batting, 56
  position for fielding, 86
  pulling the head (flaw), 76
headfirst slide, 151
health concerns, 11
heckling, 5
helmet
  moving from batter's box, 143
Hernandez, Orlando, 137
hitting
  situational, 60
hook slide, 150–151
hop
  types of on ground balls, 83

ice, 37, 122
  and pitching arm, 122
inflammation, 37
injury, 11
  shoulder, 13

Jeter, Derek, 48
Jobe exercises, 15
Jobe, Frank, 15
Johnson, Randy 125
Jordan, Al, 1, 12
Jordan, Michael, 8

knuckles
  in batting grip, 45, 65–66
  lining up the, 46
Kung Fu drill, 78

Lasorda, Tommy, 39
Lau, Charlie, 55
leading off
  a base, 148–149
Little League World Series, 5
Lombardi, Vince, 4
long toss, 36

Martin, Billy, 3
mechanics
    of hitting, 63
    of pitching, 124, 135
    of throwing, 32
morale, 7

palm
    position for batting, 54, 74
parents, 10
    meeting with, 155
Patriot, The, 28
pine tar, 45
pitch
    count, 123
        by age, 123
    off-speed, 128
pitching
    batting practice, 160
    falling off mound (flaw), 136
    grips for, 124
    mechanics, 124, 135
    practicing, 162–163
    teaching, 162
plate coverage, 42
plate discipline, 41
playing time, 6
pop up
    deciding who catches, 110
positioning
    for double play, 96, 98
    for fielders, 81
    for on-deck hitter, 144
practice
    batting, 158
    first of season, 157
    for pitchers, 163
    length of, 163
    organizing, 11, 155
Pujols, Albert, 48

"reading"
    batted ball, 107–109
    pitcher prior to stealing, 148
relay throws
    from outfield, 91–92, 107
release point
    pitching, 128, 138
Rivera, Mariano, 132
Rodriquez, Alex, 5

rotation of ball
    pitching, 136
rotator cuff, 14, 24, 122, 130, 137
    exercises for strengthening, 14

Saving the Pitcher (book), 14
Schmidt, Mike, 48, 55
second baseman
    on double-play, 98, 102
Sheffield, Gary, 64
shortstop
    on double-play, 95–96, 101
shoulder
    exercise, 21
    injury, 13
    position
        for hitting, 70, 76
        for throwing, 29, 87
situational hitting, 60, 160
sliding
    into a base, 150
    into home plate, 144
    pop-up, 150
soft hands mitt, 103, 115
stance, see also *football*
    balanced, 65
    batting, 41–43, 48
"stepping in the bucket" (flaw), 70
stretches, 15, 158
stretching
    for two players, 20
    with surgical tubing, 18
stride, batting, 49, 67
strike zone, 41–42
swing
    direction, 53
    length, 52

taking a pitch, 41
throwing
    from outfield, 112
    in double play, 101
    in fielding, 86
    mechanics of, 32
    relay, 91
thumb
    position of for pitching, 124–125
    position of for throwing, 26
Tommy John surgery, 15
two-seam grip, 25, 124
    and pitching, 124

umpire, 2
   arguing with, 2–3
upper-cutting on swing (flaw), 73

Valenzuela, F., 137
Visquel, Omar, 102

warm-up, see *stretches*

Weaver, Earl, 3
Williams, Ted, 40
wind-up, 125, 137
wrist
  in batting, 54
  in throwing, 33
  rollover (flaw), 54
    correcting, 74
  strengthening device, 75

MARC SHOENFELT is the founder and president of B2B Baseball, a youth baseball instructional business based in Lancaster, Pennsylvania. While in college, he played shortstop for the University of Louisiana at Monroe and Mansfield University. While at Mansfield, his team won two state and regional championships, advancing to the College World Series both years. Marc is a public school teacher, and in 2001 won the Amerihost Teacher of the Year Award for his work with children. Currently he acts as director of the Atlantic League Lancaster Barnstormer Summer Camps, and speaks nationally on baseball instruction. To contact Marc, log onto www.B2Bbaseball.com.